CISTERCIAN STUDIES SERIES: NUMBER ONE-HUNDRED TWENTY-FOUR

Sebastian Brock

THE LUMINOUS EYE

© Copyright C.I.I.S.

First published in 1985 by C. I. I. S., 294, Corso Vittorio Emmanuele, IV Piano, 00186 Rome. Revised edition published by Cistercian Publications, 1992.

The work of Cistercian Publications is made possible in part by support from Western Michigan University to the Institute of Cistercian Studies.

Available in the United States from the publisher
Cistercian Publications (Distribution)
Saint Joseph's Abbey
Spencer, Massachusetts 01562

Ephrem of Edessa *c.* 306–373

Library of Congress Cataloging-in-Publication Data

Brock, Sebastian P.
    The luminous eye : the spiritual world vision of Saint Ephrem / by Sebastian Brock.
        p.   cm. — (Cistercian studies series ; no. 124)
    Based on a series of lectures given by the author at the Pontifical Oriental Institute in Rome, April 1984.
    Originally published: Rome : Center for Indian and Inter-Religious Studies, 1985.
    Includes bibliographical references and index.
    ISBN 0–87907–524–4 (alk. paper). — ISBN 0–87907–624–0 (pbk. : alk. paper)
    1. Ephraem, Syrus, Saint, 303–373.   I. Title.   II. Series.
BR65.E636B76   1992
270.2'092—do20   92–6340
                                                                       CIP

Printed in the United States of America

For Helen

CONTENTS

PREFACE

1. INTRODUCTION 13

    Saint Ephrem as a Meeting Point between
    East and West 13
    Life 15
    Writings 17
    Ephrem's Triple Heritage 18
    Mode of Procedure 21

2. SAINT EPHREM'S THEOLOGICAL
    APPROACH 23

    The Poet as Theologian 23
    Some Basic Concepts and Themes 25
        Creator–Creation 26
        The Hidden and the Revealed 27
        The Primacy of Faith 29
        The Two Times 29
        The One and the Many 30
        The Pattern of Salvation 31
        Free Will 34
        The Value of the Body 36
    Imagery 38
        The Divinity as Fire 38

Clothing 39
Conception and Birthgiving 39
The Eye, Light and Mirror 39
Medical Imagery 40
Other Images 40
The Three Modes of Divine Self-revelation 40
The Prerequisites for Theological Enquiry 43
The Interpretation of Scripture 46

3. THE LADDER OF SYMBOLS:
   DIVINE DESCENT 53

Types and Symbols 53
The Garment of 'Names' 60

4. THE LADDER OF SYMBOLS:
   HUMAN ASCENT 67

The Initial Response 67
The Luminous Eye 71
Symbols Perceived 79

5. THE ROBE OF GLORY 85

The Primordial Robe 86
The Recovery of the Robe 87
The Baptism of Christ and Christian Baptism 90
The Wedding Garment 94

6. THE MEDICINE OF LIFE 99

The Medicine of Life 99
The Coal of Fire 103
The Pearl 106
Incarnation and Epiclesis 108

7. THE BRIDAL CHAMBER OF THE HEART 115

Israel as the Betrothed 116
The Church as Bride 122
Mary as Bride 126
The Bridal Chamber of the Heart 127

8. THE ASCETIC IDEAL: SAINT EPHREM AND
   PROTO-MONASTICISM 131

   Syrian 'Proto-monasticism': A Forgotten 131
   Tradition Motivation 139

9. SAINT EPHREM AMONG THE FATHERS 143

   Saint Ephrem and the Greek Fathers 143
   Saint Ephrem and the Cappadocian Fathers 145
   Divinization (theosis) 148
   Saint Ephrem and Later Monastic Tradition 154

10. SAINT EPHREM TODAY 159

   Saint Ephrem as a Representative of Asian
   Christianity 159
   Poetry as a Vehicle for Theology 160
   The Interpretation of Scripture within the
   Context of Faith 161
   Saint Ephrem's Ecological Vision 164
   The Role of the Feminine 168
   Conclusion 172

NOTES 175
SELECT BIBLIOGRAPHY 183
INDEXES 195
   Biblical References 195
   Passages in Ephrem 197
   Syriac and Greek Writers 202
   Names and Subjects 204
   Greek, Hebrew, and Syriac Terms 208

PREFACE

Each year a series of public lectures on some aspect of Eastern Christianity is held in Rome, in honour of the late Syro-Malabar scholar Fr Placid Podipara, under the auspices of the Centre for Indian and Inter-Religious Studies (C.I.I.S.). It was out of one such series of 'Placid Lectures', given in April 1984 at the Pontifical Oriental Institute in Rome, that the present book was born. In the course of its ten chapters (which represent the original lectures in only slightly altered form) I have attempted to offer to the general reader a few glimpses into the exciting spiritual vision of one of the truly great saints of early Christianity, the poet Saint Ephrem the Syrian. If to many people today he remains a relatively unknown figure, this is because his writings are for the most part not easily accessible to the non-specialist; this is unfortunate, for much of what he has to say is still remarkably relevant over sixteen centuries after his death. If this little book helps in a small way to make Saint Ephrem better known, then it will have fulfilled its main purpose.

The lectures were originally published by the C.I.I.S. in 1985, and they are here reprinted, with the gracious permission of the present Director of the C.I.I.S., the Reverend Dr Augustine Thottakara, CMI. I have taken the opportunity to make a few small revisions (mainly in the notes), to bring the bibliography up to date, and to add some indexes.

My warm thanks go to the Reverend Dr Albert Nambiaparambil, CMI who, as former Director of the C.I.I.S., initially invited

11

me to give the lectures and who provided me with this challenging subject; I only fear that I have failed to do justice to the magnitude of the topic.

MODE OF CITATION

Ephrem's hymns are cited by the title of the hymn cycle (e.g. Faith = Hymns on Faith) + number of the hymn within that cycle + stanza number. Prose works are cited either by section numbers, or by page number of the edition; details of the editions used, and of the available translations, will be found in Section A of the Select Bibliography. Ephrem's poetry is often very tightly packed, and since stanzas often have to be quoted without the benefit of their immediate context, I have sometimes felt it necessary to give somewhat expanded translations. Where the original Syriac terms are quoted, a simplified form of transcription has been adopted.

Oxford, August 1989

1

INTRODUCTION

SAINT EPHREM AS A MEETING POINT
BETWEEN EAST AND WEST

OVER THE COURSE OF THESE PAGES we shall be exploring the thought and spiritual vision of a fourth-century Church Father who amply deserves to stand side by side with his better known contemporaries, Saint Athanasius, Saint Gregory of Nazianzus, Saint Basil and Saint Gregory of Nyssa. Yet many people, to whom these four are familiar enough names, will have only a very faint idea of who Saint Ephrem was; indeed they may never even have heard of him at all. Why should this be so?

Two main reasons for this state of affairs suggest themselves: firstly, Saint Ephrem wrote in Syriac and not in Greek or Latin, and so his writings are much less accessible than might otherwise have been the case; and secondly, his most important work is in poetry, and since we do not expect to find serious theology expressed in poetic form, we tend not to take seriously as a theological thinker someone who does happen to put forward his theological vision through the medium of poetry. Ironically, it is precisely these two reasons which have led to the comparative neglect of Saint Ephrem that make him a writer of particular significance today.

The subtitle of this book (which represents the title under which these lectures were originally given) contains an ambiguity: is it to be understood as Saint Ephrem's spiritual vision of the world, or his vision of the spiritual world? In fact the ambiguity is a deliberate one, for it is not a case of either the one or the other interpretation being correct; rather, both are correct, and our exploration will be both of his spiritual vision of the world around us, and of his vision of the spiritual world. But why does the fact that Ephrem wrote in Syriac and that he expressed his theology in poetry make him a writer with something relevant to say in our present condition?

We may begin by dealing briefly with the second point, theology in poetry, since it is one to which we shall return at more length in Chapter Two. Anyone who has gone through a western educational system is likely to think of theology as being above all connected with dogmatic 'definitions'. Ephrem's approach to theology, however, avoids—indeed abhors—definitions, which he regards as boundaries (Latin *fines*) that impose limits; his own method, by contrast, is to proceed by way of paradox and symbol. This difference of approach, it should be emphasized at the outset, does not prevent Ephrem from being a theologian with a very profound sense of orthodox belief.

Let us return, then, to the other question posed just now: what is so significant about the fact that Ephrem wrote in Syriac and not in Greek or Latin? Syriac is of course a Semitic language, a dialect of Aramaic, which Christ himself spoke, and in which the Gospel will first have been preached, before it came to be written down in Greek.

Although early Syriac Christianity received its written Gospels from Greek, translated into Syriac, it nevertheless developed, during the early centuries of its existence, in a Semitic milieu that was, outside the richer upper classes, as yet comparatively little hellenized. From the fifth century onwards, however, such had become the prestige of the Greek world and of Greek ways of thinking and conducting theological discourse, that from about AD 400 onwards no Syriac writer fails to come under strong Greek influence of one sort or another.[1] Saint Ephrem, however, belongs to before this date, to the least hellenized period of Syriac Christianity, and accordingly he, and his older contemporary Aphrahat, constitute what is virtually our only evidence of any literature that emanates from a truly Semitic form of Christianity.

One might at first suppose that this simply makes Ephrem and Aphrahat into historical curiosities, solely of interest to the historian of early Christianity. But this is not the case, and it is only in the light of the subsequent history of mainstream Christianity, for the most part tied up with the course of the Roman Empire and the subsequent history of Europe, that early Syriac Christianity takes on its true significance, for here is a genuinely Asian Christianity which is free from the specifically European cultural, historical and intellectual trappings that have become attached to the main streams of Christianity with which we are familiar today.

Saint Ephrem's importance, then, lies in the fact that he is the one major writer who is a representative of Semitic-Asian Christianity in its as yet unhellenized-uneuropeanized form. Yet at the same time, even though Saint Ephrem is at a very considerable remove from his contemporaries Saint Athanasius, Saint Basil and the two Saints Gregory in language, in modes of expression, and in thought patterns, he is nonetheless essentially at one with them in his understanding of the mystery of the Trinity and the Incarnation. This is an aspect to which we shall be returning in Chapter Nine.

Saint Ephrem is thus a writer who can pre-eminently serve as a link and meeting point between European Christianity on the one hand, and Asian and African Christianity on the other. For those whose Christian tradition is of European background, Ephrem provides a refreshing counterbalance to an excessively cerebral tradition of conducting theological enquiry, while for Asian and African Christians Ephrem is the one great Church Father and theologian whose poetic writings will be readily accessible, without requiring any prior knowledge of Greek philosophical terminology and tradition.

LIFE

Who then was Saint Ephrem? Although we have quite a lot of sources claiming to tell us about his life, most of these are late and full of legendary additions; this applies above all to the Life of Saint Ephrem, which must belong to the mid sixth century— nearly two hundred years after his actual lifetime. As a result there is in fact not very much that one can say with real certainty about his life though it is quite likely that we do have the exact date of his death preserved, the 9th of June 373.

The few details about his life that are reasonably certain will not take long to outline. On the evidence of his own writings Ephrem was probably born of Christian parents (the biography's claim that his father was a pagan priest who threw his son out of the house for becoming a Christian is clearly a product of later hagiographical imagination). We do not know when he was born; 'c. 306' which is the figure usually given nowadays, is just a reasonable guess.

Except for the last ten years of his life Ephrem lived in Nisibis (modern Nuseybin on the border between southeast Turkey and northeast Syria); there he served as deacon and catechetical teacher in the local church, under the leadership of four remarkable bishops. A baptistery, built by one of these, Bishop Vologeses, in 359–60, still stands today and provides us with a tangible link with Saint Ephrem, who must have witnessed its construction and worshipped in it.

Nisibis was an outpost of the eastern Roman Empire, but in 363, after the emperor Julian's death in battle in Mesopotamia, the town was ceded to the Persians in the ensuing peace treaty. The Christian population of the town seems to have been evacuated as part of the terms of the treaty, and Ephrem eventually ended up in Edessa, some hundred miles further west, modern Urfa in southeast Turkey, the home of Syriac (which early Syriac writers call Urhaya, the Aramaic dialect of Urhay = Edessa). It was probably only in Edessa that Ephrem first encountered the full force of the fierce theological controversies that were ragingat the time, involving the followers of Marcion, Bardaisan, Arius, Eunomius, the Anomoeans, the Manichaeans and many others.

The one well-documented piece of information about Ephrem during the last ten or so years of his life, at Edessa, concerns a famine that took place there shortly before his death; during this Ephrem played a major role in organizing relief for the poor.[2] He will have been approaching the age of seventy at the time.

As we shall see in Chapter Eight, Ephrem was never formally a monk, as later tradition portrayed him. He does, however, seem to have been closely associated with a native Syrian form of what may be called 'proto-monasticism', and it is very likely that he did in fact lead some sort of consecrated life.

Ephrem probably did not know Greek, or at most only a little; he is, however, quite aware of the general tenor of theological discussion in the Greek-speaking world. He was *not* hostile to Greek culture as such, and he even has a couple of allusions in his poems to classical mythology. In this context it is important to remember that when he speaks of the need to reject 'the poison of the *Yawnaye*', the term *Yawnaye* should not simply be translated 'Greeks', for it refers primarily to *pagan* Greeks. Ephrem in fact uses the term *Yawnaye* in exactly the same sense that Greek-speaking Christians of his time used the term *Hellenes*, meaning 'pagans', rather than 'Greeks'.

Later tradition has Ephrem travel to Cappadocia to visit Saint Basil, and to Egypt to visit Saint Bishoi. Neither of these visits is historical, though on a symbolic level they can be said to convey a certain truth, as will emerge from Chapter Nine.

WRITINGS

An enormous number of writings in many different languages has come down to us attributed to Ephrem. A large proportion of them, however, are certainly not by our Ephrem (this applies in particular to the Greek texts under his name); many others are of doubtful authenticity, but a fair number still remain which can be safely accepted as genuine. For present purposes I shall base myself almost entirely on the last category, writings whose authenticity is generally acknowledged by scholars today.

These works fall into four categories, two in prose and two in verse. A few works are preserved only in an Armenian translation. (For details reference should be made to the Bibliography at the end).

Straight prose:

—polemical works;
—prose commentaries on biblical books, the most important of which are those on Genesis and on the Diatessaron (or Gospel harmony).

Artistic, or rhythmic, prose:

—the 'Discourse on our Lord';
—Letter to Publius (mainly on the Last Judgement).

Verse homilies (*memre*), in 7+7 syllable couplets

—Six *memre* on faith;
—*memre* on the destruction of Nicomedia in an earthquake (AD 358).

The majority of the other *memre* attributed to Ephrem are of very doubtful authenticity.

Hymns (*madrashe*):

—A dozen or so cycles, containing varied numbers of hymns, are preserved. These *madrashe* are stanzaic poems, employing over fifty different syllabic patterns; they were meant to be sung, and the names of the melodies survive, but not the original music. The *madrashe* were collected together into hymn cycles sometime after Ephrem's death, and these took their titles from the first group of hymns that they contained. The cycles come down to us in a number of sixth-century manuscripts, and these form the basis of Dom Edmund Beck's editions in the Louvain Corpus of Oriental Christian Writers. We know the names of some further cycles which are no longer extant or which only survive in an incomplete form. It is on the *madrashe* or hymns (of which we have well over four hundred) that Ephrem's reputation as a poet hangs, and it is in these hymns that some of his most profound spiritual insights are to be found. Accordingly it will be from this stanzaic poetry that most of the quotations in the ensuing chapters will be drawn.

EPHREM'S TRIPLE HERITAGE

In his writings Ephrem shows himself to be an heir to three main cultural traditions: he is an heir of ancient Mesopotamian tradition. This can be seen in a number of different ways, and here I select just two of the most prominent.

In a half dozen or so of his poems Ephrem employs the literary genre of the precedence dispute, consisting of a formalized debate between two participants, each arguing for his or her own superiority. The genre goes right back to Sumerian literature in Ancient Mesopotamia, and it was to have a long future, after Ephrem's time, both in Syriac and in many other different literatures. Ephrem himself has precedence disputes of this sort notably between Death and Satan and between Marriage and Virginity. Something of the flavour of these disputes can be gained from the following extract, taken from the opening of the fifty-second Nisibene Hymn:[3]

1. I heard Death and Satan loudly disputing which was the stronger of the two amongst humanity.

Refrain: Praise to You, Son of the Shepherd of all, who has saved His flock from the hidden wolves, the Evil One and Death, who had swallowed it up.

2. Death has shown his power in that he conquers all. Sin has shown his guile in that he makes everyone sin.

3. (Death) Only those who want to, O Evil One, listen to you, but to me they come, whether they will or not.

4. (Satan) You just employ brute force, O Death, whereas I use traps and cunning snares.

5. (Death) Listen, Evil One, a cunning person can break your yoke, but there is none who can escape from mine.

6. (Satan) You, Death, exercise your strength with the sick, but I am the stronger with those who are well.

Ephrem furthermore inherited a number of themes and symbols from Ancient Mesopotamia;[4] one which he employs a great deal is the term Medicine of Life (or Salvation), *sam ḥayye* in Syriac,

corresponding to *sam balaṭi* in Akkadian, with the same meaning. Very often Ephrem refers the term to Christ himself ('the
Medicine of Life flew down from on high',*Discourse 3*), or to the
Eucharist ('Your body is the Medicine of Life', *Nisibis 76:6*). It is
interesting to discover that quite a number of titles which Ephrem
gives to Christ have their origins in the religious literature of Ancient Mesopotamia.

Ephrem is an heir to Judaism. This can be seen in two different respects. Firstly, Ephrem, like any other Christian, inherited
the Jewish Bible, which became the Christian Old Testament.
Ephrem's writings show an intimate familiarity with the Bible,
and his hymns in particular are packed with subtle verbal allusions
(which he clearly expected his listeners and readers to catch).

Secondly, and more significantly, Ephrem is also an heir to
many Jewish traditions that are only to be found outside the Bible,
in post-biblical Jewish literature, in the Targumim (Aramaic translations of the Bible) and Midrashim (homiletic expositions). These
will have reached Ephrem indirectly, and perhaps by way of oral
tradition, for there is absolutely no evidence that he drew directly
on Jewish literary sources in either Aramaic or Hebrew. Many
of these non-biblical Jewish traditions are not to be found in any
other Christian source apart from Ephrem and some other early
Syriac writers.

One such theme ultimately of Jewish origin, which is all-
pervasive in Ephrem's writings, is that of the creative tension between God's Grace (*ṭaybuta*) and Righteousness (*kenuta*):[5]

> The scales of Your balance are Grace and Righteous-
>   ness:
> how and when they are balanced, You alone know.
> Though they may not seem to be balanced, they are
>   balanced all the same
> since they are not divided against the One Lord of all.
>   (*Faith 12:4*)

The roles accorded by Ephrem to Grace and Righteousness correspond in a general fashion to the functions of the 'aspect',

or 'measure, of mercy' (*middat ha-raḥamim*) and the 'aspect', or 'measure, of judgement' (*middat ha-din*) in Rabbinic writings.

Ephrem is also heir to the Greek world. As was mentioned earlier, even though Ephrem probably did not read Greek directly, he was nevertheless generally aware of the theological climate of Greek-speaking Christianity.[6] Moreover, some of his biblical imagery and allusions may derive ultimately from the Greek, rather than the Syriac Bible. It is also possible that a few Greek Christian writers may have already been translated into Syriac during Ephrem's lifetime: this could, for example, be the case with some of Eusebius' works, such as the *Ecclesiastical History* and *Theophania* (the latter preserved complete only in Syriac translation), and Titus of Bostra's *Treatise against the Manichaeans*.

These three very different cultural traditions, Ancient Mesopotamian, Jewish and Greek, find a meeting point in Ephrem to an extent that cannot be paralleled in any other early Christian writer. Once again Ephrem can be seen to provide a bridge between East and West, between Asia and Europe.

MODE OF PROCEDURE

Although Saint Ephrem has a very coherent and well thought out theological vision, he does not ever express this vision in any systematic form. Indeed, as we shall see, his approach dislikes any kind of systematization, and is essentially dynamic and fluid in character. This of course means that the attempt I am making, to present something of his thought in a more or less systematized form, is like forcing someone into a straightjacket. I shall, however, try to avoid imposing upon Ephrem categories that are foreign to his way of thinking; instead, my aim has been to allow his own writings to dictate the choice of subjects to be treated, and then in every case I have attempted to extract and distil, as far as I have been able, the essence of his thought and its basic structures and underlying presuppositions. Quotations from Ephrem's own works will accompany the exposition throughout, and at times these extracts may be fairly extensive.

Needless to say, it has been necessary to be very selective in the choice of topics to be covered, and many important areas of Saint Ephrem's theological vision have had to be passed over in silence.

2

SAINT EPHREM'S
THEOLOGICAL APPROACH

THE POET AS THEOLOGIAN

TO MANY THE IDEA OF THE POET as a theologian may seem
like a contradiction in terms: poets may indeed at times
touch on theological themes, but we do not normally expect theologians to express their theological vision in poetry. The
loss is ours, for over the course of centuries of the study of theology we have all too often narrowed down the ways in which we
think theology should be conducted, and we have lost sight of a
famous aphorism of Saint Ephrem's younger contemporary Evagrius, with which our saint would heartily have agreed: 'If you
are a theologian, you will pray in truth; if you pray in truth, you
will be a theologian'. Accordingly we should not be surprised to
find good theology in a poet like Ephrem who clearly 'prayed
in truth'.

Saint Ephrem's approach serves as a much needed antidote to
that tradition of theologizing which seeks to provide theological
definitions, Greek *horoi*, or boundaries. To Ephrem, theological
definitions are not only potentially dangerous, but they can also
be blasphemous. They can be dangerous because, by providing
'boundaries', they are likely to have a deadening and fossilizing
effect on people's conception of the subject of enquiry, which is,
after all, none other than the human experience of God. Dogmatic 'definitions' can moreover, in Ephrem's eyes, be actually

23

blasphemous when these definitions touch upon some aspect of God's Being: for by trying to 'define' God one is in effect attempting to contain the Uncontainable, to limit the Limitless.

Since Ephrem was living at the time when Arianism in its various forms was seen as the prime source of danger for the Church, much of his polemic on this topic focuses on the eternal Generation of the Son from the Father. Those who placed this Generation inside time, and thus on our side of the ontological gap (or 'chasm', as Ephrem calls it)[1] between Creator and created, could reasonably treat the subject as one which the created human intellect could investigate. To Ephrem, however, and to the orthodox in general, this was a double blasphemy: the various Arian factions had not only located the Son on the wrong side of the ontological gap, but they had then been led on by this initial error into attempting a rational definition of the Son's Generation from the Father.

If 'definitions' of faith appear to confine within boundaries the boundless God, how then should the theologian try to proceed? The search for theological definitions, a heritage from Greek philosophy, is of course by no means the only way of conducting theological enquiry. Ephrem's radically different approach is by way of paradox and symbolism, and for this purpose poetry proves a far more suitable vehicle than prose, seeing that poetry is much better capable of sustaining the essential dynamism and fluidity that is characteristic of this sort of approach to theology.

How does this theology of paradox work? To illustrate in a simple way the basic difference between what one may call the philosophical approach to theology, with its search for definitions, and the symbolic approach, one may visualize a circle with a point in the centre, where the point represents that aspect of God under enquiry. The philosophical approach seeks to identify and locate this central point, in other words, to define it, set boundaries to it. The symbolic approach, on the other hand, attempts no such thing; rather, it will provide a series of paradoxical pairs of opposites, placing them at opposite points around the circumference of the circle; the central point is left undefined, but something of its nature and whereabouts can be inferred by joining up the various opposite points, the different paradoxes, on the circle's circumference. The former procedure can be seen as providing a static understanding of the centre point, while the latter offers an understanding that remains essentially dynamic in character.

Among Ephrem's favorite paradoxes, when he is talking of the Incarnation, are 'the Great One who became small', 'the Rich One who became poor' (based on 2 Corinthians 8:9), 'the Hidden One who revealed himself'. Here, for example, is how he tries to convey something of the mystery of the birth of the divine Word from Mary: (Ephrem at first addresses Christ)

> Your mother is a cause for wonder: the Lord entered
> her
> and became a servant; He who is the Word entered
> —and became silent within her; thunder entered her
> —and made no sound; there entered the Shepherd of
> all,
> and in her He became the Lamb, bleating as He came
> forth.
>
> Your mother's womb has reversed the roles:
> the Establisher of all entered in His richness,
> but came forth poor; the Exalted One entered her,
> but came forth meek; the Splendrous One entered her,
> but came forth having put on a lowly hue.
>
> The Mighty One entered, and put on insecurity
> from her womb; the Provisioner of all entered
> —and experienced hunger; He who gives drink to all
> entered
> —and experienced thirst: naked and stripped
> there came forth from her He who clothes all.
>
> (*Nativity 11:6–8*)

SOME BASIC CONCEPTS AND THEMES

In Ephrem's writings one encounters a number of basic concepts and recurring themes, some of which we need to be aware

of at the outset; they constitute the grammar, as it were, of his
theological language.

Creator-Creation

Ephrem is constantly aware of the sharp divide between Creator
and creation. In one of the Hymns on Faith (69:11) he speaks
of this ontological gap as a 'chasm', reflecting the term used in
the Parable of Dives and Lazarus (Luke 16:26); across this chasm
'what is made cannot reach its Maker' (*Faith 30:2*). This means
that created 'natures' are incapable of saying anything about the
divine nature (*ibidem*).

Now the precise location of this 'chasm' between Creator and
created was, as we have seen, a matter of dispute in the fourth
century. Ephrem emphatically locates the Divine Word on the far
side of this ontological 'chasm', while all angelic beings belong,
together with corporeal ones, to the side of creation.

Linked to this consciousness of the inability of any created thing
to cross this 'chasm' to the Creator is an awareness (which Ephrem
shares with many of the Fathers) that the intellect that has knowledge of something must be greater than the object of its knowledge. On such an understanding, anyone who claims that it is
possible to know (and so describe) God is at the same time implying that the human intellect is capable of 'containing' God, the
uncontainable. Hence Ephrem's horror of attempts to 'investigate'
('*aqqeb*) or 'pry into' (*bṣa*) God's nature:

> Whoever is capable of investigating
>   becomes the container of what he investigates;
> a knowledge which is capable of containing the Om-
>   niscient
>   is greater than Him,
> for it has proved capable of measuring the whole of
>   Him.
> A person who investigates the Father and Son
>   is thus greater than them!
> Far be it, then, and something anathema,

that the Father and Son should be investigated,
while dust and ashes exalts itself!

(*Faith 9:16*)

Ephrem's recurrent warnings against 'investigation' and 'prying' into the divine 'hiddenness' should not lead us to suppose that his attitude is anti-intellectual. Far from it, for the human intellect, as he sees it, has plenty of scope within creation, where its role is to search out the types and symbols available there to provide it with glimpses of understanding of divine reality. It is only when the intellect seeks to cross the ontological 'chasm' that it becomes reprehensible. The proper area for intellectual enquiry lies in the places where God has revealed himself in creation, the *galyata*, 'revealed things'. Thus in the Hymns on Faith (8:9) Ephrem states:

There *is* intellectual enquiry in the Church,
investigating what is revealed:
the intellect was not intended to pry into hidden things.

This brings us on to our next topic, the creative tension present in Ephrem's frequent use of the terms 'revealed' and 'hidden'.

The Hidden and The Revealed

When using these terms 'hidden' and 'revealed' Ephrem will be employing one of two totally different perspectives. Most frequently he will employ what we may term the human perspective: God is hidden, except in so far as he allows himself to be revealed. This human experience of God's hiddenness (*kasyuta*) is only possible through God's various instances of self-revelation. For a created being experience of all these different individual self-manifestations of God will never add up to a full revelation of God's hiddenness; the revelation is always partial. This means that this human perspective is essentially subjective: each individual will approach God's hiddenness by way of a different set of *galyata*, or points of revelation.

Needless to say it is at the Incarnation that God's hiddenness is

before His death and resurrection in linear time, came to be understood in early Syriac tradition as the fountainhead and source of all Christian baptism.

The concept of sacred time is also important in Ephrem's hymns from two other standpoints.

In the first place it sheds light on his understanding of the significance of the descent of Christ into Sheol, the underworld of the dead. Whereas Christ's incarnate life on earth is an entry into historical time and space, Palestine of the first century, the descent into Sheol is concerned solely with sacred time and space: it is Christ's entry into both past and future time, and it is not bounded by geographical space. The descent thus has a structural importance in the scheme of salvation equal to that of the earthly life of Christ, in that it obviates the accusation of particularity that might otherwise arise—the accusation that Christ's work was limited by considerations of historical time and geographical space. The purpose of the doctrine of the descent of Christ into Sheol is precisely to show that the incarnation effects *all* historical time and *all* geographical space. To achieve this, however, it has to speak in terms of sacred time and sacred space, and accordingly the descent can only be described in a story-like and mythopoeic manner—something that Ephrem does with great dramatic effect in the second half of the cycle of Nisibene hymns.

The second standpoint from which the concept of sacred time is of importance for the understanding of Ephrem's thought concerns the tension between the Christian's experience of the sacraments of baptism and the eucharist in historical time, and their full realization at the eschaton. Because the paradisiacal life of the eschaton belongs to sacred time, it is possible for it to be experienced, in varying degrees, by individuals already in historical time on earth. This is something to which we shall return in Chapter Six.

The One and The Many

The freedom with which, in Semitic thought, the individual can merge into the collective, and the collective into the individual, is familiar to all students of the Old Testament. This way of thinking is very much present in Ephrem's writings, above all when he is talking of Adam: 'Adam' in Ephrem may refer to the individual of the Genesis narrative or to the human race in general, or indeed to both simultaneously. Adam is Everyman. The Pauline reference to Christ as the 'last Adam' (1 Corinthians 15:45) thus takes on particular significance for Ephrem: on several occasions he specifies that it is 'Adam's body', or 'the body of mortal Adam' that the Word puts on at the Incarnation; it is 'the body of Adam which proves victorious in Christ' (*Crucifixion 5:11*). Or again Ephrem may use the term 'Adam' in order to link the effect of the Incarnation both with primordial and with eschatological time:

> Blessed is He who put on Adam,
> leaped up and made him pass over
> on the Wood into Paradise.

(Fast 2:4)

Exactly the same creative tension between the individual and the collective can be observed in Ephrem's understanding of the relationship between the individual Christian and the Church. As we shall discover in Chapter Seven, it is the Church who is betrothed to Christ at Christ's own baptism in the Jordan, whereas at each Christian baptismal ceremony it is the individual soul that is betrothed.

The pattern of salvation

Although we shall be returning to this topic in more detail later on, it will be helpful if at the outset we are aware of Ephrem's understanding of the intended role of humanity in creation. Outlined schematically he sees the following pattern of salvation history.

Adam and Eve (humanity) had been created in an intermediary state, neither mortal nor immortal: it was the exercise of their free will (*ḥeruta*, 'freedom') over the instruction not to eat of the fruit of the Tree of Knowledge which would decide the matter: if they kept the command (Ephrem emphasizes how small it was), God would have rewarded them, not only with the fruit of the Tree of Knowledge, but also with the fruit of the Tree of Life, and they would have become immortal and been divinized. As it was, of course, they failed to obey the commandment, and as a result were both expelled from Paradise and became subject to death (which Ephrem sees as a merciful deliverance from the terrible consequences of their disobedience).

The entire aim of God henceforth has been to effect the means for Adam/humanity to return to Paradise, while still respecting the awesome gift of free will with which humanity has been endowed. But it is not just to the intermediary state of primordial Paradise that God wishes humanity to return: in the eschatological Paradise humanity is to receive the gift of divinity from the Tree of Life that God had originally intended for the primordial Adam and Eve.

Primordial and eschatological Paradise belong to sacred time and space, and so they are ever present and directly connected with the pattern of salvation for every individual human being. The expulsion from Paradise, on the other hand, represents the transition from sacred to historical time and space; it is the entry into the fallen world of geographical space and historical time with which we are all too familiar.

Ephrem perceives a detailed pattern of complementarity between the processes of fall and restoration: all the individual details of the Fall are reversed, so that we are presented with a series of contrasted types, with Adam/Christ and Eve/Mary as protagonists. Salvation history can thus be described as a process of healing which extends both back to the reaches of primordial time, and down to the depths of the fallen human state. At the Incarnation God the Word clothes himself not only with 'Adam' and 'Adam's body', but also 'our body', 'humanity', 'our weak state'.

The pattern of complementarity begins with Mary's wise questioning of the angel, counterbalancing Eve's foolish failure to question the serpent. In Ephrem's hands this already traditional contrast between Mary's obedience and Eve's disobedience has given rise to the image of Satan pouring poison into Eve's ear—just as in Shakespeare's Hamlet Claudius is represented as having done to

Hamlet's father while asleep; and, contrasting with this, we also find Mary described as having conceived through her ear:[2]

> Just as from the small womb of Eve's ear
> Death entered in and was poured out,
> so through a new ear, that was Mary's,
> Life entered and was poured out.
>
> (*Church 49:7*)

This pattern of complementarity becomes most close-knit at the Passion, as the following extracts will illustrate:

> In the month of Nisan our Lord repaid
> the debts of that first Adam:
> He gave His sweat in Nisan in exchange for Adam's
> sweat,
> the Cross, in exchange for Adam's Tree.
> The sixth day of the week corresponded to the sixth
> day of creation,
> and it was at 'the turn of the day' (Genesis 3:8)
> that He returned the thief to Eden.
>
> (*Church 51:8*)

Or, in greater detail:

> Our Lord subdued His might, and they seized Him
> so that His living death might give life to Adam.
> He gave His hands to be pierced by the nails
> in place of that hand that had plucked the fruit;
> He was struck on the cheek in the judgement hall
> in return for that mouth that had devoured in Eden.
> Because Adam had let slip his foot,
> they pierced His feet.
> Our Lord was stripped naked so that we might be
> clothed in modesty;
> with the gall and vinegar He made sweet
> that bitter venom that the serpent had poured into hu-
> man kind.
>
> (*Nisibis 36:1*)

The same pattern is applied to the resurrection:

Christ's tomb and the Garden are symbols of Eden
where Adam died a hidden death,
for he had fled and hidden himself among the trees
as though he had entered a tomb and been covered
     over.
The Living One, once entombed, has now arisen in
     the Garden
and raised up that Adam who had fallen in the Garden:
from the tomb of the garden did Christ bring Adam in
     glory
into the marriage feast of the Garden of Paradise.

(Crucifixion 8:13)

Free will

Human free will (*ḥeruta*, literally 'freedom') plays an extremely important role in Ephrem's thought. A hymn devoted to the subject (*Heresies 11*) has the response 'Lord, you have magnified the small body above all other created things by endowing it with free will'. As we have already seen, God created Adam in an intermediate state in order that he might reward him with a higher one if Adam chose, of his own free will, to keep the commandment:

The Just One did not wish to give Adam the crown
     for nothing,
even though He allowed him to enjoy Paradise without
     toil.
God knew that if Adam wanted he could win the prize:
it was because the Just One wished to enhance him,
for, although the rank of supernal beings is great
     through grace,
the crown for the proper use of man's free will is no
     small thing either.

(Paradise 12:18)

It was through Adam's misuse of free will that he was ejected from Paradise, and it is because of their correct use of this gift that the saints are rewarded:

Blessed is He who wove the commandments
so that through them free will might be crowned;
blessed is He who has multiplied the righteous,
the witnesses who shout out concerning free will.

(*Heresies 11:4*, end)

God 'could have forced us to please him without any trouble to
himself, but instead he toiled by every means so that we might act
pleasingly to him of our own free will' (*Faith 31:5*).

Noah's generation provided Ephrem with a prime example of
the use and abuse of free will:

Take the example of Noah: he is able to rebuke
all his contemporaries, for if they had wanted
they too could have prospered,
since the strength of our human free will
was the same in them as in Noah.

(*Church 3:9*)

Nor is the activity of free will confined to the moral sphere: it
is entirely up to us whether we respond to the various forms of
God's self-revelation: 'our own free will is the key to Your treasury'
(*Church 13:5*).

Free will is present in everyone in the same measure, even
though it may not appear very obviously in those who—of their
own free will—have enslaved themselves to sin. Ephrem explains
this by means of a medical analogy:

The nature of our free will is the same in everyone:
if its power is weak in one, it is weak in all,
if its power is strong in one, it is the same in all.

The nature of sweetness seems sweet to someone in
    good health,
but bitter to anyone sick; so too it is with free will:
it is sickly with sinners, but in good health with the
    righteous.

When someone wants to test the nature of sweetness
he does not test or try it out in the mouths of people
    who are ill:
it is the healthy mouth that provides the furnace to
    assay tastes.

When again someone wants to test the power of free
    will
he should not test it in the impure, who are sick with
    ugly deeds;
no, a pure person, who is healthy, should provide the
    furnace in which to assay it.

If a sick person should say to you that the taste of
    sweetness
is bitter, observe how strong his sickness has grown,
so that he has abused the sweetness, that source of de-
    lights.

If again some impure person should say to you
that the power of free will is feeble, observe how he
    has cut off his hope
by impoverishing free will, the treasure that humanity
    possesses.

(*Church* 2:18–23)

THE VALUE OF THE BODY

Ephrem is at a far remove from those platonizing or dualistic
tendencies, characteristic of certain trends of early Christianity,
that sought to denigrate the value of the body. The starting point
for his own positive attitude is the fact that the body is part of
God's creation and so should not be despised, let alone thought
of as in any way evil. But Ephrem has three further important
considerations.

First is the evidence of Scripture itself: commenting on 1 Corinthians 6:19, 'Do you not know that your bodies are a temple

of the Holy Spirit who dwells within you', Ephrem points to the honour which God himself pays to the body by making it 'a dwelling place and habitation of the Trinity' (*Commentary on the Pauline Epistles*, p. 62 = p. 59; he goes on to quote John 14:23); and later on, commenting on 2 Corinthians 5, he says 'Just as our bodies became worthy to be the dwelling of his Spirit, so he makes them worthy at the end to put on eternal glory' (*Commentary on the Pauline Epistles*, p. 96 = p. 96). Ephrem elsewhere speaks of the human body as having become God's new temple, replacing the Temple on Mount Sion (*Heresies 42:4*).

Secondly, the very fact that God 'put on a body' (*Nativity 9:2* and often elsewhere) indicates that there is nothing unclean or unworthy about the body. And finally, the Eucharist provides Ephrem with similar evidence of the worth of the body; in the following extract he is arguing against a group of Christians who hold the body to be impure but accept the Eucharist:

> If our Lord had despised the body
> as something unclean or hateful and foul,
> then the Bread and the cup of Salvation
> should also be something hateful and unclean to these
>   heretics;
> for how could Christ have despised the body
> yet clothed himself in the Bread,
> seeing that bread is related to that feeble body.
> And if he was pleased with dumb bread,
> how much more so with the body endowed with
>   speech and reason?
>
> (*Heresies 47:2*)

Exactly the same thing is indicated by the fact that God allows the Holy Mysteries, his own Body and Blood, to be consumed by human bodies:

> God would not have mingled His Mysteries in the body
>   had it originated from the Evil One.
>
> (*Heresies 43:3*)

Body and soul are thus equally important in Ephrem's eyes; they simply have different roles to play:

> The body gives thanks to You
> because You created it as an abode for Yourself,
> the soul worships You
> because You betrothed it at Your coming.

(Heresies 17:5)

As we shall see in Chapter Seven, the body provides the bridal chamber where the bride, the soul, meets the heavenly Bridegroom.

IMAGERY

The newcomer to Saint Ephrem's poetry will at once be struck by the wealth of his imagery. Here it will suffice to single out just a few of his favorite images so that they can be readily recognized as such in the various passages we shall have occasion to quote.

The divinity as fire

Ephrem very frequently describes the divinity as fire; thus at the Incarnation 'Fire entered Mary's womb, put on a body and came forth' (*Faith* 4:2). Fire is the 'symbol of the Spirit' (*Faith* 40:10), and at the Eucharist 'the Spirit is in the Bread, the Fire in the Wine' (*Faith* 10:8). In the case of Old Testament sacrifices the descent of fire from heaven was an indication of divine acceptance (1 Kings 18:38; *Faith* 10:13), while at the Eucharist 'the Fire of Mercies has become a living sacrifice for us', Fire which we actually consume (*Faith* 10:13).

> This divine Fire has a double aspect, for it can both
> sanctify and destroy:
> Blessed are you, my brethren,
> for the Fire of Mercy has come down
> utterly devouring your sins
> and purifying and sanctifying your bodies.

(Epiphany 3:10)

The double aspect of the action of fire also features in a different sort of context when Ephrem employs the metallurgical imagery of the 'furnace', as for example:

> Let Job uncover for you the impudence of Satan:
> how he asks and beseeches the Just One for permission
> to test out your minds in the furnace of temptations.
> This is what the Abominable One said:
> 'No silver has ever been assayed without fire;
> falsehood will be put to shame, what is true will get
>   due praise'.
>
> *(Paradise 12:11)*

Clothing

Perhaps the most frequent of all Ephrem's images is that of putting on and taking off clothing.[3] As we shall see in Chapter Five, it is by means of clothing imagery that Ephrem is able to present his readers with a cohesive picture of salvation history. In keeping with this, his favorite term for the Incarnation is 'He put on a body' (following the earliest Syriac translation of *esarkothe*, 'He became incarnate', in the Nicene Creed).

Conception and Birthgiving

Another extremely common image is that of conception and birthgiving; no doubt the frequency with which this feminine imagery is met is just another indication of Ephrem's feeling for, and understanding of, women—an aspect we shall be considering in Chapter Ten. It also fits in with the general emphasis, characteristic of early Syriac Christianity as a whole, on baptism as a rebirth, rather than as a death and resurrection, following the Johannine, rather than the Pauline, conceptual model.[4]

The Eye, Light and Mirror

Ephrem was clearly fascinated by mirrors—not the glass mirrors we know today, but the metal ones that had to be kept polished in order to reflect the light and the image of the beholder.[5] Use of the images of the mirror, light and the eye allow Ephrem to explore the optics, as it were, of spiritual perception. This is a topic we shall be considering in Chapter Four.

Medical Imagery

Medical imagery is of course already common in the Bible, but in Ephrem's hands it undergoes considerable developments which would repay special study. Here I merely single out the title of Christ as 'the good' or 'the wise Doctor', the bearer of 'the Medicine of Life'. (It is just possible that the title 'the good Doctor' deliberately reflects the Syriac text of the apocryphal letter of King Abgar of Edessa to Jesus, as found in the Teaching of Addai).[6]

Other Images

Imagery from agriculture, from archery, from sailing, from commerce and travel, and from many other spheres of life are likewise to be found everywhere in Ephrem's hymns. And it is perhaps because his poetry abounds in these images drawn from everyday life, that it retains a freshness and immediacy even for the modern reader.

We should finally note an unexpected feature in Ephrem's writings, his sense of humour. This he usually exploits in a self-deprecatory fashion, especially in the final stanza of a poem, as for example at the conclusion of a particularly beautiful hymn on the Eucharist:[7]

> Look, Lord, my lap is now filled with the crumbs
>   from Your table*   *Mt 15:27
> there is no more room in the folds of my garment,
> so hold back Your gift as I worship before You;
> keep it in Your treasure house in readiness to give
> it us on another occasion.
>
>   (*Faith 10:22*)

THE THREE MODES OF DIVINE SELF-REVELATION

If the created human intellect is incapable of crossing the onto-logical 'chasm' that exists between Creator and creation, how can anything be learnt of God? Ephrem's answer is that nothing at all would be possible if God had not himself taken the initiative and crossed the chasm in order to reveal himself in various ways to his creation:

> Had God not wished to disclose Himself to us
> there would not have been anything in creation
> able to elucidate anything at all about Him.

> *(Faith 44:7)*

We can isolate three main ways by which Ephrem understands this process of divine self-revelation to take place: through types and symbols which are present in both Nature and in Scripture; through the 'names', or metaphors, which God allows to be used of himself in Scripture; and above all of course in the Incarnation.

Types and symbols serve as pointers. From the subjective human perspective a type or symbol can be seen as a revelation of some aspect of the divine hiddenness (whether or not that aspect may one day be more fully revealed). From the objective divine perspective the reverse is the case: some aspect of divine reality lies hidden in the type or symbol. Ephrem employs a variety of different words (including the Greek word *tupos*), but by far the most common term is *raza* (plural *raze*), 'secret, mystery, symbol'. Symbol and reality (*shrara*, literally 'truth') are intimately linked, for inherent in the symbol, or *raza*, is the 'hidden power', or meaning (*hayla kasya*) of the reality. Ephrem shares this 'strong' understanding of the term 'symbol' with many of the Greek and Latin Fathers, and it should be stressed that this understanding is very different from that current in modern English usage, where the symbol is usually sharply differentiated from what it symbolizes. It is also significant that the plural *raze*, 'mysteries', is the standard term in Syriac for the Eucharist (compare the Greek *ta mysteria*).

Clearly Ephrem's strong understanding of what a symbol is leads him to a very positive attitude to the two main vehicles for symbols, the biblical text (and above all the Old Testament) and the natural world round about him. Scripture and Nature (*ktaba* and *kyana*) indeed constitute God's two witnesses, as required by Jewish law (John 8:17); they are

the witnesses which reach everywhere,
are found at all times,
are present at the every moment,
rebuking the unbeliever who denies the Creator.

(Paradise 5:2)

Wherever you turn your eyes, there is God's symbol
whatever you read, there you will find His types.

(Virginity 20:12)

For Ephrem, both Scripture and Creation are replete with God's symbols and mysteries, symbols which may point vertically, as it were, to his trinitarian Being, or horizontally to his incarnate Son. How these operate we shall be exploring in the next two chapters.

In the Scriptures, however, God does not only reveal something of himself by means of symbols, he also clothes himself in human language, 'He puts on names', as Ephrem frequently expresses it. For the most part the names that God 'puts on' are only metaphors, borrowed from the human condition. Ephrem sees this as an act of immense condescension on the part of God, who comes down to meet humanity on its own terms, in its own language; he is insistent that we, for our part, should not abuse this graciousness by supposing that these 'names' or metaphors are to be understood literally. Since all this is something that we shall be looking at in more detail both in the final section of this chapter and in the next chapter, no more need be said about this second mode of God's self-revelation at present.

Finally we have the fullest self-revelation of God at the Incarnation, when God the Word 'put on a human body', thus providing a fitting climax to this earlier 'incarnation into human language', already to be encountered in the Old Testament:

> God's Majesty that had clothed Itself in all sorts of
>   similitudes
> saw that humanity did not want to find salvation
>   through this assistance,
> so He sent His Beloved One who, instead of the bor-
>   rowed similitude
> with which God's Majesty had previously clothed Itself,

clothed Himself with real limbs, as the First-born,
and was mingled with humanity:
He gave what belonged to Him and took what belonged to us,
so that this mingling of His might give life to our dead
state.

(Heresies 32:9)

THE PREREQUISITES FOR THEOLOGICAL ENQUIRY

Theology, like any other intellectual pursuit, can take on three different forms, depending on the attitude of mind present in the person setting out on the path of enquiry. In the first place the mind may seek to dominate and subjugate the object of its enquiry. Such an attitude has characterized much scientific and other enquiry from the time of Francis Bacon onwards. Whether rightly or wrongly, Ephrem saw this as the basic attitude of many 'heretical' thinkers of his own time: in the field of theology, in particular, such intellectual pride is utterly abhorrent to him.

A second approach takes on what at first seems a much more acceptable form, a form that is typical of much theological enquiry today: here the mind sets out to study the object of it enquiry in as dispassionate and 'scientific' a way as possible. It is an approach which in many spheres is of course very fruitful, and it is one that Ephrem implies that he himself tried—but found wanting:

Turn me back to Your teaching: I wanted to stand back,
but I saw that I became the poorer. For the soul does
not get any benefit
except through converse with You.

(Faith 32:1)

The third approach, which is Ephrem's, is that of engagement, an engagement above all of love and wonder. Whereas the second approach involves only a one–way movement, from the mind to the object of enquiry, this third approach is a two–way affair, involving a continual interaction. Only by means of such an

interaction of love can human knowledge of divine truth grow.
Ephrem continues in the same hymn:

> Whenever I have meditated upon You
> I have acquired a veritable treasure from You;
> Whatever aspect of You I have contemplated,
> a stream has flowed from You.
> There is no way in which I can contain it:
>
> Your fountain, Lord, is hidden
> from the person who does not thirst for You;
> Your treasury seems empty
> to the person who rejects You.
> Love is the treasurer
> of Your heavenly treasure store.
>
> *(Faith 32:2–3)*

The way in which we perceive both God and the created
world about us thus depends on our basic attitude and approach,
whether we perceive them as objects of enquiry somehow separate from ourselves (in which case we can either try to dominate them, or treat them more on a par with ourselves), or
whether we see ourselves as irrevocably involved in the object
of our enquiry and, in the case of theology, are willing actually to participate in the mystery concerned. Ephrem is in no
doubt that this last way is not only the sole truly acceptable
way, but also the sole possible one where any knowledge of God
is sought.

An essential concomitant of this initial attitude of engagement
and participation is a sense of wonder and awe. Such a sense of
wonder is all pervasive in Ephrem's writings: 'Blessed is He who
has astounded our thought by the simple things of life', he exclaims *(Faith 43, refrain)*. But it is wonder above all at the supreme
manifestation of God's love for humanity when He Himself 'put
on humanity' *(Fast 3:6; Heresies 35:7)*: 'It is a matter of wonder
that God has bent down to dust' *(Faith 46:11)*.

Wonder gives birth to love and praise, and 'corresponding to
the extent of our love, we shall acquire, through praise, life that

has no measure' (*Nisibis 50:5*). Indeed, to live without praise is to live as though dead:

> While I live I will give praise, and not be as if I had
>   no existence;
> I will give praise during my lifetime, and will not be
>   as someone dead among the living.
> For the man who stands idle is doubly dead,
> the earth that fails to produce defrauds him who
>   tills it.
>
> (*Nisibis 50:1*)

And without love Truth cannot be attained:

> Truth and love are wings that cannot be separated,
> for Truth without Love is unable to fly,
> so too Love without Truth is unable to soar up:
> their yoke is one of harmony.
>
> (*Faith 20:12*)

The third line of this stanza brings us to a further matter of importance for Ephrem: the starting point for any kind of theological enquiry is to know what areas of theology can be investigated by the human intellect and what areas cannot; in other words, one must know where exactly to locate the ontological gap between Creator and creation. This means that if one does not start out from an orthodox theological position, one will make mistakes from the very beginning: wrong initial conceptions will only lead to further error. This, as we have already seen, was Ephrem's basic complaint with the various Arian positions.

Similarly, it is only in the light of orthodox belief that Scripture can be properly interpreted:

> The keys of doctrine which unlock all Scripture
> have opened up before my eyes the book of creation,
> the treasure house of the Ark, the crown of the Law.
> It is Scripture in its narrative which, above all its companions,
> has perceived the Creator and transmitted His works:

beholding all His handiwork it has made manifest
the objects of His Craftsmanship.

(Paradise 6:1)

THE INTERPRETATION OF SCRIPTURE

It will be helpful at this point to anticipate some of the ground
which will be covered in the next two chapters and to examine
briefly Ephrem's understanding of how Scripture should be interpreted. It is a topic to which we shall also return, in a wider
context, in Chapter Ten.

What God has allowed to be said of himself in the Bible is,
for Ephrem, a primary source for any human knowledge of God.
The 'names' of God and the various types and symbols in Scripture
constitute meeting points between God and humanity: God in his
divine condescension has lowered Himself to the level of human
understanding. From the human side, if advantage is to be taken
of this opportunity, offered by God, of a way towards a knowledge
of Himself, two things are essential, as we have already learnt: in
the first place we must not make the ungrateful mistake of taking
the names and metaphors used of God in Scripture literally; and
secondly, the attitude of the reader must be one of receptivity and
openness: if he approaches Scripture with the wrong attitude, or
with his own preconceptions, then not only will he fail to gain
from Scripture any knowledge of God, but he may actually be led
astray.

Scripture may be said to possess both an exterior and an interior meaning; the exterior belongs to the sphere of what we
could call historical reality, the interior to that of spiritual reality:
both coexist, just as the humanity and divinity do in the incarnate
Christ. The parallelism which Ephrem sees between God's two
incarnations, first into human language when 'He put on names'
in Scripture, and then the Incarnation proper, throws important
light on his understanding of Scripture and the need he sees for
the presence of faith in its interpretation. In the absence of faith
Jesus of Nazareth remains merely a historical figure, his humanity is all that is visible to the beholder; only when the beholder

also looks with the inner eye of faith does the divinity of Christ become apparent. So too with Scripture: where there is no inner eye of faith, all that is visible is the exterior, historical, meaning of Scripture—what the Fathers generally call 'the letter'. This is the perspective of academic biblical scholarship, and as that discipline has developed in the past century, so this historical perspective has become very much more nuanced. But for Ephrem this perspective is not enough, since it only concerns historical reality: just as only the eye of faith can move from the historical person of Jesus to the incarnate Christ, so too with Scripture only the eye of faith can penetrate inward to discover something of the interior meaning, of spiritual reality:

> The Scriptures are laid out like a mirror,
>   and he whose eye is lucid sees therein the image of
>   Truth.
>
> *(Faith 67:8)*

Ephrem, in his role as theologian, is naturally primarily interested in penetrating to the interior meaning of Scripture, a realm only explorable by means of discernment *(purshana)* and this inner eye of faith. Indeed he stresses that to stop at Scripture's outward statements about God and to take them literally is both dangerous—in that it will lead to misconceptions about God's nature—and at the same time a sign of utter ingratitude for, and misunderstanding of, God's condescension in allowing himself to be spoken of in human language at all:

> If someone concentrates his attention
> solely on the metaphors used of God's majesty,
> he abuses and misrepresents that majesty
> by means of those metaphors
> with which God has clothed Himself for humanity's
>   own benefit,
> and he is ungrateful to that Grace
> which has bent down its stature to the level of human
>   childishness;
> even though God has nothing in common with it.

He clothed Himself in the likeness of humanity
in order to bring humanity to the likeness of Himself.

(Paradise 11:6)

We should not suppose that Ephrem has no interest in, or attaches no importance to, the outward historical meaning of Scripture: this exterior sense has just as important a function as has the humanity of Christ. Outward historical meaning and inner spiritual meaning of Scripture are as intimately intermingled and linked as are body and soul in the human person and humanity and divinity in Christ. What is important for Ephrem is a proper understanding of the interrelationship of, and interaction between, all these pairs. To deny the value of the one and concentrate solely on the other is dangerous and misguided, whichever way round it be. Thus Ephrem's quarrel with the Jews was that they looked only at the humanity of Jesus, and only at the exterior meaning of the Scriptures, refusing to penetrate further to the interior sense, which, according to Ephrem, would have led them to faith in Christ:[8]

The Jews are put to shame
for they failed to study and seek out
the reason for the Law;
instead they took up and dissolved
the meaning of the commandments,
clothing themselves without any understanding
in the sounds of the words,
for they did not labour to acquire
that furnace of thought by which they might assay
the truth and real meaning of Scripture.

(Heresies 50:4)

Ephrem is clearly aware that there is a sharp difference between the nature of outer historical, and inner spiritual, exegesis of Scripture. The former, being confined to the sphere of creation, is finite: interpretations can, at least in theory, be fixed and conclusive. Spiritual exegesis, on the other hand, operates under quite a different set of rules, and it is essentially fluid and the number of possible interpretations is not finite. The 'names' which God has put on in Scripture, and the symbols and types to be found everywhere in both Nature an Scripture, are as it were windows, or rather, just peepholes, to 'Truth'.[9] In the first place, to see through these peepholes at all, the essential prerequisite is the eye of faith; but once given its initial presence, this eye of faith can operate in different ways with different people, or indeed in different ways with the same person, but at different times. A person whose inner eye is 'darkened' will not see much in Scripture, but one whose eye is 'lucid and clear' will behold a great deal: 'Everyone corresponding to the measure of his discernment has perceived Him who is Great above all' (Nativity 4:200).

Such, however, is the immense wealth of the 'Truth', or spiritual reality, for the eye of faith to gaze upon in Scripture, that no single individual is capable of taking in everything. There are thus infinite 'interpretations', that is descriptions of what the inner eye beholds, possible:

> If there only existed a single sense for the words of Scripture, then the first commentator who came along would discover it, and other hearers would experience neither the labour of searching, nor the joy of finding. Rather, each word of our Lord has its own form, and each form has its own members, and each member has its own character. Each individual understands according to his capacity and interprets as it is granted him.
>
> (Commentary on the Diatessaron 7:22).

It is not a case of one interpretation being right and another wrong (as can often be the case with historical exegesis); rather, an interpretation is valid in so far as it is meaningful to a particular individual at a particular time. Error enters in when one person claims that his spiritual interpretation is the only one possible, or that the interior and exterior meanings of a particular passage are mutually incompatible. This is emphatically not the case: the two types of interpretation, historical dealing with the exterior sense, and spiritual dealing with the interior, are concerned with two quite different modes of reality, or 'Truth', and the one truth or reality does not cancel out the other: the two modes can coexist happily side by side.

For obvious reasons Ephrem is only rarely concerned with historical interpretation, and where he does operate on this level, what he has to say is not very satisfactory, judged by the much more sophisticated techniques of historical interpretation that have been developed over the past century. But wherever his main concern is with the interior, spiritual, meanings of Scripture (and this is his usual concern), there his insights are still capable of striking the sympathetic modern reader as often possessing great profundity.

In this section I have been extracting what seems to me to be the essence of Ephrem's understanding of Scripture and its interpretation, and it is time to let him speak himself again directly. In this passage on the multiplicity of inner meanings in Scripture Ephrem begins by addressing Christ:

> Who is capable of comprehending the extent of what is to be discovered in a single utterance of Yours? For we leave behind in it far more than we take from it, like thirsty people drinking from a fountain.
>
> The facets of His word are more numerous than the faces of those who learn from it. God depicted His word with many beauties, so that each of those who learn from it can examine that aspect of it which he likes. And God has hidden within His word all sorts of treasures, so that each of us can be enriched by it from whatever aspect he meditates on. For God's word is the Tree of Life which proffers to you on all sides blessed fruits; it is like the Rock which was struck in the Wilderness, which became a spiritual drink for everyone on all sides: 'They ate the food of the Spirit and they drank the draft of the Spirit'.
>
> Anyone who encounters Scripture should not suppose that the single one of its riches that he has found is the only one to exist; rather, he should realize that

he himself is only capable of discovering that one out of the many riches which exist in it.

Nor, because Scripture has enriched him should the reader impoverish it. Rather, if the reader is incapable of finding more, let him acknowledge Scripture's magnitude. Rejoice because you have found satisfaction, and do not be grieved that there has been something left over by you. A thirsty person rejoices because he has drunk: he is not grieved because he proved incapable of drinking the fountain dry. Let the fountain vanquish your thirst, your thirst should not vanquish the fountain! If your thirst comes to an end while the fountain has not been diminished, then you can drink again whenever you are thirsty; whereas if the fountain had been drained dry once you had had your fill, your victory over it would have proved to your own harm. Give thanks for what you have taken away, and do not complain about the superfluity that is left over. What you have taken off with you is your portion, what has been left behind can still be your inheritance.

(Commentary on the Diatessaron I:18–19)

3

THE LADDER OF SYMBOLS:
DIVINE DESCENT

WE HAVE ALREADY SEEN in the previous chapter how it is possible to distinguish, in Saint Ephrem's thought, three main modes of divine self-revelation, by means of types and symbols in both Nature and in Scripture, through the 'names' which God has put on in Scripture, and in the Incarnation when He actually 'put on our body'. It is the first two of these modes of revelation which we will be exploring in a little more detail here.

TYPES AND SYMBOLS[1]

God's dealing with humanity has, as its ultimate aim, the restoration of humanity to the paradisiacal state, a state that in fact will be even more glorious than that of Adam and Eve before the Fall. To achieve this 'God wearies himself by every means so as to gain us' (*Faith 31:4* end), but because he has given us free will, he never imposes himself on us: there is no question of any force or compulsion being used, seeing that

> Any kind of adornment that is the result of force
> is not genuine, for it is merely imposed.
> Herein lies the greatness of God's gift,
> that someone can adorn himself of his own accord,
> in that God has removed all compulsion.
>
> *(Nisibis 16:11)*

It is due to this respect paid by God to the free will with which he has endowed humanity that we are never compelled by him in any of the means by which he seeks to draw fallen humanity back to himself. Thus types and symbols are definitely *not* to be seen as proof texts whose aim is to compel assent; rather, they are just invitations, offering the possibility of acquiring some knowledge of divine reality. The choice whether or not to accept them—and likewise whether or not to accept Jesus of Nazareth as the Son of God—is left as a matter for the exercise of human free will: to accept is always a choice guided by the freedom of faith, and not by the compulsion of proof. Grace never imposes itself by force *(Nisibis 16:6)*.

Ironically, if compulsion is to be found anywhere, it can be said that it is God's own love for humanity that compels Him to take the initiative in providing the opportunities by which humanity can return to Him. A poem containing a lively dialogue between Mary and the angel Gabriel, and attributed to Ephrem, opens with the words:[2]

> The Power of the Father, compelled by His love,
> descended and dwelt in a virgin womb.

The purpose of the types and symbols available in Nature and Scripture is thus to entice humanity back from its fallen state by offering innumerable glimpses of the glorious divine reality; through these instances of divine self-revelation humanity is offered the opportunity of growth in spiritual awareness:

> Lord, You bent down and put on humanity's types
> so that humanity might grow through Your
> self-abasement.
>
> *(Faith 32:9)*

At the same time, if the matter is considered from the perspective, not of humanity, but of objective divine reality, symbols and types can be said to serve as a veil to protect humanity from the overpowering brightness of God's full revelation:

> With the ray that comes from Himself
> Christ softened His wondrous might:

it is not that He grew weak at all,
it was to please us that He softened it, for our sakes.
We have represented Him as a 'Ray',
even though this is not His likeness,
for there is nothing that can accurately depict Him.
He allows Himself to be depicted with various like-
    nesses,
so that we may learn of Him, according to our ability.
Thanksgiving be to His blessed assistance!

(Faith 6:3)

When Ephrem explores the infinite number of symbols and
types in Nature and Scripture we must be constantly aware that,
although human understanding of them is essentially fluid and
variable, what they all point to is an objective reality that Ephrem
calls 'Truth'. Furthermore, the presence in the types and symbols
of what he calls the 'hidden power', or 'meaning' lends to them
some sort of inner objective significance of reality, which is different from that outer reality which the scientific observer would call
objective. The presence of this 'hidden power' accords a deeper
meaning and significance to whatever outward vehicle that symbol may be attached to, even though that vehicle (which may be a
person or an object) will normally not be aware of the indwelling
presence of this 'hidden power':

Lord, Your symbols are everywhere,
yet You are hidden from everywhere.
Though Your symbol is on high,
yet the height does not perceive that You are;
though Your symbol is in the depth,
it does not comprehend who You are;
though Your symbol is in the sea,
You are hidden from the sea;
though Your symbol is on dry land,
it is not aware what You are.
Blessed is the Hidden One shining out!

(Faith 4:9)

Types and symbols are to be found everywhere, simply as a result of the world having been created by God; they are pointers to his existence and creative activity. 'Creation gives birth to Christ in symbols, as Mary did in the flesh' *(Virginity 6:8)*. They are of course only observable by the eye of faith, and the clearer that eye is, the more symbols will become visible, and each individual symbol will also become more meaningful.

The existence of these hidden symbols thus provides a cohesive substructure of strands linking and connecting together every part of creation. Since they all point to some aspect of divine reality, their presence in God's two witnesses, Scripture and Nature, infuses new meaning into both the natural world and the Bible. Everything and every action has the potential of taking on deeper significance. Ephrem's understanding of symbols thus offers an essentially sacramental understanding of the world, and here we can recall that the plural of *raza*, 'symbol', is frequently used in the sense of 'sacraments'.

Types and symbols, then, are the means by which the interconnectedness of everything can be seen, the means by which meaning can be found infused in everything. It is a dynamic and exciting way of looking at the world—and one that is profoundly ecological.[3]

Symbols are multi-faceted: they have no one single meaning. If we take the example of the pearl, to which Ephrem devotes a famous group of hymns,[4] we can prosaically state that, for Ephrem, the pearl is a symbol of the Kingdom, of faith, of Christ, his virgin birth, his crucifixion, and so on; the one meaning does not exclude the others: the pearl simply serves as a window opening into all sorts of different aspects of 'Truth', it is an invitation to, and starting point for, meditation:

> Even though Your symbol may be small,
> yet it is a fountain of further mysteries.
>
> *(Faith 4:10)*

Ephrem sees a continuous dialectic between the one divine reality and the many symbols:

> Single is Your nature, but many are the ways of inter-
> preting it.
>
> *(Faith 10:3)*

First we have the movement from the One to the many: so infinite
is the single nature of God that it can be described in infinitely
different ways, can be represented by infinitely different symbols.
And then we have the movement back from each of the many
symbols to the One. And here too each individual symbol is itself
capable of whole wealth of different meanings, in that that particular aspect of the divine reality to which it points is infinitely
rich in itself.

So far we have been primarily concerned with Ephrem's general
view of the purpose and function of types and symbols. A few
extracts may now serve to illustrate the various ways in which
Ephrem handles them in his poetry.

Not surprisingly the vast majority of types and symbols which
Ephrem discovers latent in the Old Testament point forward to
the advent of Christ: what was hidden in the symbol is revealed
in Christ. Christ is the 'sea' into which symbols pour *(Virginity
9:12)*; 'Fulfilment entered and actually put on the symbol which
the Holy Spirit had woven for Him' *(Unleavened Bread 6:22)*.

Ephrem has a whole series of poems on the typological parallels
and contrasts between the passover lamb (Exodus 12) and Christ
the True Paschal Lamb. In this extract Ephrem draws out the
contrasts between the single Exodus effected by the passover lamb
and the double one, from both Satan and Death, achieved by the
True Lamb:[5]

> Listen to the simple symbols that concern that Passover,
> and to the double achievements of this our Passover.
> With the Passover lamb there took place for the Jewish
>   people
> an Exodus from Egypt, and not an entry.
> So with the True Lamb there took place for the Gen-
>   tiles
> an Exodus from Error, not an entry.

With the Living Lamb there was a further Exodus too,
for the dead from Sheol, as from Egypt.

(Unleavened Bread 3:5–8)

In the next passage, however, we are pointed forward not only to
Christ and his crucifixion, but also to baptism:

Noah's Ark marked out by its course the sign of its
   Preserver,[6]
the Cross of its Steersman and the Wood of its Sailor
who has come to fashion for us a Church in the waters
   of baptism:
with the three-fold name He rescues those who reside
   in her,
and in place of the dove, the Spirit administers her
   anointing
and the mystery of her salvation. Praise to her Saviour.
His symbols are in the Law, His types are in the ark,
each bears testimony to the other: just as the ark's re-
   cesses
were emptied out, so too the types in Scripture
were emptied out; for by His coming he embraced
the symbol of the Law, and in His churches He brought
   to completion
the types of the ark. Praise to your coming!

(Faith 49:4–5)

In this poem the dove which brings Noah the olive leaf (Genesis
8:11) points forward to the Holy Spirit and baptismal anointing, but in another hymn the olive leaf takes on a different role,
this time representing olive oil (meshha), the symbol of Christ
(Meshiha):

Let oil in all its forms acknowledge You in Your entirety
for oil gives rest to all.
The olive served Christ, who gives life to all,
depicting Him in its abundance, its branches and leaves:
with its branches it praised Him—through the
   children*

*Jn 12:13

with its abundance—through Mary★　　　　　　　　★*Jn 12:3*
with its leaf again, through the dove which served Noah
    His type;
with its branches it depicted the symbol of His victory,
with its abundance it depicted the symbol of His
    dying,★　　　　　　　　　　　　　　　　　★*Jn 12:7*
with its leaf it depicted the symbol of His resurrection,
the Flood disgorging it, as Death disgorged Christ.
The face which gazes on a vessel filled with oil
sees its reflection there, and he who gazes hard
sets his spiritual gaze thereon
and sees in its symbols Christ.
And as the beauty of Christ is manifold,
so too the olive's symbols are manifold.
Christ has many facets, and the oil acts as a mirror to
    them all:
from whatever angle I look at the oil,
Christ looks out at me from within it.

　　　　　　　　　　　　　　　(Virginity 7:13–14)

Oil provides an example of a symbol that is shared by both
Scripture and Nature. A final passage will illustrate the sort of
way in which Ephrem discovers symbols latent everywhere in the
world around him. In this hymn he compares the growth of faith
to the growth of a bird, and in particular Ephrem observes that,
in order for the bird to be able to fly it will have to open its wings
'in the symbol of the Cross'; he then goes on:

　　But if the bird gathers in its wings,
　　　thus denying the extended symbol of the Cross,
　　then the air too will deny the bird:
　　the air will not carry the bird
　　unless its wings confess the Cross.

　　　　　　　　　　　　　　　　(Faith 18:6)

In the next chapter we shall see how humanity too needs to open
its wings of faith, like the bird, if it is to fly upwards and ascend
the ladder of symbols which is there awaiting it.

THE GARMENT OF 'NAMES'

Ephrem offers his readers a developed theology of names which in several ways remarkably anticipates that found in the treatise on Divine Names in the dionysian corpus. Several hymns are entirely devoted to the subject, but perhaps none is more important than Hymn Thirty-One of the cycle on Faith, which is worth quoting at some length. In stanzas Six and Seven (the last two quoted here) Ephrem, with an undertone of subtle humour, compares God's efforts to teach humanity about himself to those of someone who is attempting, with the aid of a mirror, to teach a parrot to talk.

> Let us give thanks to God who clothed Himself in the
>   names of the body's various parts:
> Scripture refers to His 'ears', to teach us that He listens
>   to us;
> it speaks of His 'eyes', to show that He sees us.
> It was just the names of such things that He put on,
> and, although in His true Being there is not wrath or
>   regret,
> yet He put on these names too because of our weakness.
>
> Refrain: Blessed is He who has appeared to our human
>   race under so many metaphors.
>
> We should realize that, had He not put on the names
> of such things, it would not have been possible for Him
> to speak with us humans. By means of what belongs
>   to us did He draw close to us:
> He clothed Himself in our language, so that He might
>   clothe us
> in His mode of life. He asked for our form and put
>   this on,
> and then, as a father with His children, He spoke with
>   our childish state.
>
> It is our metaphors that He put on—though He did
>   not literally do so;

He then took them off—without actually doing so:
   when wearing them,
He was at the same time stripped of them.
He puts one on when it is beneficial, then strips it off
   in exchange for another;
the fact that He strips off and puts on all sorts of
   metaphors
tells us that the metaphor does not apply to His true
   Being:
because that Being is hidden, He has depicted it by
   means of what is visible.

In one place He was like an old man and the Ancient
   of Days,
then again, He became like a hero, a valiant warrior.
For the purpose of judgement He was an old man, but
   for conflict He was valiant.
In one place He was delaying; elsewhere, having run,
He became weary. In one place He was asleep,
in another, in need. By every means did He weary
   Himself so as to gain us.

For this is the Good One, who could have forced us
   to please Him,
without any trouble to Himself; but instead He toiled
   by every means
so that we might act pleasingly to Him of our free will,
   that we might depict our beauty
with the colours that our own free will had gathered;
whereas, if He had adorned us, then we would have
   resembled
a portrait that someone else had painted, adorning it
   with his own colours.

A person who is teaching a parrot to speak
hides behind a mirror and teaches it in this way:

when the bird turns in the direction of the voice which
    is speaking
it finds in front of its eyes its own resemblance reflected;
it imagines that it is another parrot, conversing with
    itself.
The man puts the bird's image in front of it, so that
    thereby it might
learn how to speak.

This bird is a fellow creature with the man,
but although this relationship exists, the man beguiles
    and teaches
the parrot something alien to itself by means of itself;
    in this way he speaks with it.
The Divine Being that in all things is exalted above all
    things
in His love bent down from on high and acquired from
    us our own habits:
He laboured by every means so as to turn all to Himself.

                                                  (Faith 31:1–7)

In this poem Ephrem is making two basic points: since humanity
cannot cross the ontological chasm and so approach God, God has
to cross it in the opposite direction first; only thus can commu-
nication be established: God has to descend to humanity's lowly
level, and address that humanity in its own terms and language.
And secondly, the whole aim of this divine descent into human
language is to draw humanity up to God.

It is written in Scripture that the Good Lord 'repented'
    and 'was weary',
for He put on our weakness; but then He turned round
    and clothed us in the names of His own majesty.

                                                  (Faith 54:8)

The names that God puts on are of two different sorts. They
may be either the 'perfect and exact names', that is, those which
indicate something of his true Being: or they may be 'borrowed

names', that is, the metaphors borrowed from ordinary human experience:

> God has names that are perfect and exact,
> and He has names that are borrowed and transient;
> these latter He quickly puts on and quickly takes off.
>
> *(Faith 44:2)*

The 'perfect names', such as 'Being', 'Creator', Father, Son and Holy Spirit, are those which are applicable at all times, and are essential to faith:

> Take care of God's perfect and holy names,
> for if you deny one of them, then they all fly away off:[7]
> each one is bound up with the other,
> they support everything, like the pillars of the world.
>
> *(Faith 44:3)*

These 'perfect names' represent for Ephrem the highest meeting point for humanity with God: they are each a revelation of God's hiddeness, but to penetrate beyond that revelation is not possible or permitted, for what lies impenetrably beyond, in the divine hiddenness, is the *qnoma*, the person or self, of God:

> Father, Son and Holy Spirit can be reached only by
>   Their names;
> do not look further, to Their Persons *(qnome)*,
> just meditate on Their names.
> If you investigate the person of God, you will perish,
> but if you believe in the name, you will live.
> Let the name of the Father be a boundary to you,
> do not cross it and investigate His nature;
> let the name of the Son be a wall to you,
> do not cross it and investigate His birth from the Father;
> let the name of the Spirit be a fence for you,
> do not enter inside for the purpose of prying into Him.
>
> *(Memra on Faith 4:129–40)*

Some of God's 'perfect names' are terms shared with humanity: Father, Son, King. Although these are names that God has 'put on'

from human language, nevertheless Ephrem sees them as applying
properly only to God, since they are terms which are eternally
applicable to Him, whereas when applied to human beings this is
only a temporal matter: no one is born already a father.[8] In the
Bible, Ephrem explains, people

> . . . have been called 'gods', but He is God of all;
> they are called 'fathers', but He is the true Father;
> they are named 'spirits', but there is the Living Spirit.
> The terms 'fathers' and 'sons' by which they have been
>   called
> are borrowed names that through grace have taught us
> that there is a single True Father
> and that He has a single True Son.
>
> *(Faith 46:12)*

The fact that these names are shared between Creator and created should not lead one to suppose that God and humanity really
have anything in common:

> Who is so stupid and stubborn as to suppose, even just
>   a little,
> that because human beings have been called by names
>   that belong to God,
> that the nature of man and of God is consequently one,
> or that, because the Lord has also been called by a name
>   appropriate to His servants,
> that we should weigh with a single comparison both
>   what is made and its Maker.
>
> When God called us 'king', using the name appropriate
>   to Himself,
> the true use remains with Him, the likeness applies to
>   us.
> But when again He called Himself by a name appro-
>   priate to His servants,
> the natural usage lies with us, but the appellation with
>   Him.

The true name needs to be recognized and the bor-
    rowed name needs to be recognized,
both in His case and in ours.

Accordingly, in His mercy, for the discerning He ac-
    corded
His various names to His creatures—not to be investi-
    gated, but to be savored and enjoyed.
So, brethren, let prying dry up and let us multiply
    prayers,
for though He is not related to us, He is as though of
    our race,
and though He is utterly separate, yet He is over all
    and in all.

(Faith 63:9–11)

It is essential not to misunderstand the character of God's 'borrowed names'. These names which He condescends to put on are
designed to draw humanity upwards: only human arrogance and
folly uses them to drag God down to the human level:

The foolish man saw only what belongs to us
and imagined that what originated from us referred to
    God.

(Faith 54:8 end)

Rather, Ephrem says elsewhere,

God has made small His majesty
    by means of these borrowed names.
For we should not imagine
    that He has completely disclosed His majesty:
this is not what His majesty actually is,
but it represents only what we are capable of:
what we perceive as His majesty is but a tiny part,
for He has shown us a single spark from it;
He has accorded to us only what our eyes can take
of the multitude of His powerful rays.

(Heresies 30:4)

At the roots of Ephrem's theology of names one can discern the idea of salvation history as following a pattern of exchange between God and humanity:

> Loving is the Lord who Himself put on our names—
> right down to the mustard seed was He abased in the
>   parable.
> He gave us His names, He received from us our names;
> His names did not make Him any the greater,
> whereas our names made Him small.
> Blessed is the person who has spread Your fair name,
>   Lord,
> over his own name, and adorned with Your names his
>   own names.
>
> *(Faith 5:7)*

This is a concept which is absolutely basic to Ephrem's thought; it is one that we have had occasion to meet in various forms already, and it is one that we shall be encountering again when we consider Ephrem's understanding of *theosis*, or divinization.[9]

4

THE LADDER OF SYMBOLS:
HUMAN ASCENT

IN EPHREM'S THOUGHT the transcendence and immanence of God are held in a continual state of tension. The Being of the Creator is utterly hidden from, and unknowable by, his creation; yet, owing to his immense love for the humanity he has created in his own image, he is immanent in the world, having made himself available, as it were, to those who choose to look for him in the right way. Ephrem expresses this insight as follows:

> In the case of the Godhead, what created being is able
>   to investigate Him?
> For there is a great chasm between him and the Creator.
> In the case of the Godhead, it is not that He is distant
>   from His possessions,
> for there exists love between Him and creation.
> None of those who try to investigate God has ever
>   drawn near to Him
> —yet He is extremely close to those who have discern-
>   ment.
>
> *(Faith 69:11–13)*

What Ephrem is saying in these three verses will by now be familiar to us: since creation cannot cross the ontological gap to the Creator, the Creator Himself crosses the chasm out of love for His creation; even so, He will only be experienced as having done so by those who seek Him with the right attitude—and this attitude is basically one of love and faith. In other words, God's love, to be experienced, must be reciprocated.

Throughout Ephrem's writings we find him contrasting two radically different attitudes and approaches: those who 'pry into' and 'investigate' divine matters, and those who seek with discernment (*purshana*). Which approach to adopt is left entirely to the choice of an individual's free will. The choice of the former approach, however, will always prove to be the outcome of pride and preconceptions,[1] while that of discernment will stem essentially from an attitude of faith, openness and love.

The wrong approach is actually counterproductive:

> A person who seeks after truth with a grudging spirit
> cannot gain knowledge even if he actually encounters
>   it,
> for envy has clouded his mind
> and he does not get any the wiser, even if he grabs at
>   that knowledge.
>
>   (*Faith 17:1*)

Preconceptions too can lead searchers astray. Ephrem illustrates these dangers from the Jewish rejection of Christ in the New Testament: the Jewish authorities had their own preconceived ideas of what the Messiah should be like, and so they rejected the true Messiah when he did not live up to their picture:

> Thus did the Jewish people dispute with Jesus with
>   questions:
> 'Who is he, and whose son, and how has he come; or
>   is he still to come?'
> And they thought that it was too difficult for a virgin
>   to give birth.
> So the elders and scribes blasphemed against him
> because they themselves had given birth to a messiah
>   who did not exist,
> a fiction of their thought, conjured up by the mind.

Rebuke your thought, do not play the adulterer, and
    father for us
a messiah who does not exist,
and so deny the one who does.
Beware lest you fashion some idol in the course of your
    investigation;
beware lest you depict in your mind something con-
    jured up by your own intellect.
Let the true Child be depicted in your thought.

                          (Faith 44:9–10)

    The correct approach, as Ephrem sees it, is to recognize the fact that if we can learn anything about God, it is only because He has 'bent down'[2] first to the level of our understanding. A proper awareness of this will result in an attitude of wonder (*tehra*), a key word in Ephrem's hymns. It is the absence of a sense of wonder that leads to 'prying and investigation'; and for this, one of the biblical examples that Ephrem cites is the case of Balaam, who failed to 'wonder' when his donkey spoke (*Faith 41:7*).
    A sense of wonder gives rise to faith, and faith is the prerequisite if any knowledge of God is to be attained. Faith is a 'second soul' to the body, and

Just as the body keeps alive by means of the soul,
so too does the life of the soul depend on faith;
if it denies, or becomes divided by doubt, it becomes
    a mere corpse.

                          (Faith 80:1)

    Ephrem illustrates this necessity for faith from the analogy of a blind person:

If a blind person, although unable to depict the sun and
    its rays
in his heart and his thought,
nevertheless tries to investigate the source of light,
how is he able and capable of seeing the sun's ray and
    offspring

except by just believing
the person who has described it to him?

If a sightless person wanted to raise difficulties,
not believing what he had heard, he would fall into ten
    thousand calamities,
all because he tried to investigate, but did not succeed.
He wanted to be proved blind in two respects:
in mind as well as in eye.
Had he been willing to believe,
then supplication to Righteousness
would have illumined his blindness.

(*Faith 65:10–11*)

Faith 'is the eye which can see hidden things' (*Church 24:3*),
and faith in turn needs to be accompanied by love and prayer.
Addressing Christ Ephrem exclaims:

You are entirely a source of amazement,
from whatever side we may seek You:
You are close at hand, yet distant—
who shall reach You?
Searching is quite unable
to extend its reach to You:
when it is fully extended trying to attain to You
then it is cut off and stops short,
being too short to reach Your mountain.
But faith gets there,
and so does love with prayer.

(*Faith 4:11*)

God's love wishes to be met by a response of human love and
desire for Him. Love has the key to the divine treasure house
(*Faith 32:3*, quoted in Chapter Two). But is not this response of
human love presumptuous, asks Ephrem? Even if it is, such love
is actually pleasing to God:

I want to be impudent in showing my love,
but I shrink from being over bold.

Which of these two attitudes do You choose, Lord?
The impudence of our love is pleasing to You,
just as it pleased You that we should steal from Your
treasure.

(*Faith 16:5*)

(The term translated here by 'impudence' is in Syriac *ḥuṣpa*, a word that will be very familiar to anyone with a knowledge of Yiddish slang: it is the *hutzpah*, the brazen cheek, of our love that is pleasing to God).

THE LUMINOUS EYE

Ephrem employs three main images to describe how faith can succeed where investigation and prying fail, images of the eye, the ear, and of the way or road. We shall just examine the first of these here.

The inner eye of the mind (*Faith 53:12*), or of the soul (*Faith 5:18*), functions by means of faith, in much the same way that the exterior, physical, eyes functions by means of light. The presence of sin darkens this inner eye by keeping out the light of faith, and so, in order that this inner eye may see properly, it needs to be kept lucid and clear.

In a delightful short poem, Hymn Thirty-Seven of the cycle on the Church, Ephrem compares Eve and Mary to the two inner eyes of the world: one is darkened and cannot see clearly, while the other is luminous and operates perfectly:

Illumine with Your teaching
the voice of the speaker
and the ear of the hearer:
like the pupil of the eye
let the ears be illumined,
for the voice provides the rays of light.

Refrain: Praise to You, O Light.

It is through the eye
that the body, with its members,

is light in its different parts,
is fair in all its conduct,
is adorned in all its senses,
is glorious in its various limbs.

It is clear that Mary
is the 'land' that receives the Source of light;
through her it has illumined
the whole world, with its inhabitants,
which had grown dark through Eve,
the source of all evils.

Mary and Eve in their symbols
resemble a body, one of whose eyes
is blind and darkened,
while the other
is clear and bright,
providing light for the whole.

The world, you see, has
two eyes fixed in it:
Eve was its left eye,
blind,
while the right eye,
bright, is Mary.

Through the eye that was darkened
the whole world has darkened,
and people groped
and thought that every stone
they stumbled upon was a god,
calling falsehood truth.

But when it was illumined by the other eye,
and the heavenly Light
that resided in its midst,
humanity became reconciled once again,

realizing that what they had stumbled on
was destroying their very life.

In passing we should observe that in this poem on the world's
two eyes it is Mary's vision which is held up as a model. She
again is the model when Ephrem turns to auditory imagery: her
listening and obedience, born out of faith, is contrasted both with
Eve's disobedience and Zechariah's lack of faith when the angel
foretold the birth of his son, John the Baptist.[3] The significance
of the role of Mary in Ephrem's theological vision is something
of which we shall see more in subsequent chapters.

The term which Ephrem uses to describe Mary's eye in this
hymn is worth dwelling on briefly, since it is an important one,
not only for Ephrem, but also for Syriac Christianity in general
(in particular in the later mystical writers such as Saint Isaac of
Nineveh). Her eye is *shaphya*, a Syriac word which has no single translation equivalent in English, but it includes 'clear, pure,
limpid, lucid, luminous'. In the Gospels the adjective is used both
of a path, clear of stones (i.e. smooth; Luke 3:5), and of the
heart (Luke 8:15). This latter usage is of particular interest; it
already occurs in the Old Syriac Gospels, where it renders Greek
kalos, 'fair, beautiful'.[4] The translator's choice of *shaphya* here
may well have been dictated by the background of the phrase
lebba shaphya, 'pure, or luminous heart', in Jewish Aramaic; in
the Palestinian Targum to Genesis 22:6, for example, we learn
that Abraham and Isaac proceed to Mount Moriah with 'a luminous heart'. Ephrem himself uses this phrase (*Church 34:3*),
but it is in connection with the inner eye that he normally employs the term *shaphya*: a luminous eye, *'ayna shaphita*, is what
the prophet Ezekiel has (*Church 11:4*), and elsewhere Ephrem
exclaims:

> Blessed is the person who has acquired a luminous eye
> with which he will see how much the angels stand in
>   awe of You, Lord,
> and how audacious is man.
>
> (*Faith 3:5*)

Furthermore 'the Luminous One' is a title which Ephrem employs a considerable number of times with reference to Christ, as, for example:

> How can I sing to You, O Luminous and Holy One?
> For it is only the mouth that is pure and luminous
> and which resembles You, Lord, that shall sing to You
> —the luminous to the Luminous One, the pure to the
>   Pure One,
> for it is his voice that is pleasing to You.
>
> (*Church 29:1*)

Ephrem uses the term *shaphya*, and the accompanying abstract noun *shaphyuta*, 'luminosity', in many other contexts as well. One which is closely connected with the optical imagery of the eye concerns the mirror. The mirror, in order to reflect the image of the person looking into it, must also be *shaphitha*, 'luminous'— that is to say, polished, seeing that mirrors in antiquity were of metal, and so had to be kept in a state of high polish if they were to function properly.

Usually in Ephrem's imaginative handling of mirror imagery we find him looking into a mirror and seeing reflected there some aspect of 'Truth', or spiritual reality. Thus, for example, Jephtha's daughter is a mirror in which the resurrection is reflected (*Nisibis 63:5*). Sometimes, however, Ephrem's attention may be focused primarily on whether or not the mirror is properly polished.

This aspect of the mirror is very prominent when Ephrem speaks of the mirror of the self—a mirror which should reflect the divine image, but which all too often has got darkened:

> One complains about a mirror if its luminosity is dark-
>   ened,
> because it has become spotted, or dirt has built up,
> covering it over for those who look into it.
>
> *Refrain*: Blessed is He who has polished our mirror.
>
> Beauty is no longer adorned in that mirror,
> blemishes are no longer reproved in its reflection.

It is a cause for offence as far as anyone beautiful is
    concerned,
seeing that their beauty gets no advantage from it,
in the form of adornments as profit.

Blemishes can no longer be rooted out with its aid,
adornments can no longer be added with its help;
the blemish that now remains is a cause for offence,
that no embellishment has taken place is a further loss:
offence and loss have met together.

If our mirror is darkened
this is altogether a source of joy to those morally ugly
in that their blemishes are no longer reproved;
whereas if our mirror is polished and illumined,
then it is our free will that has been adorned.

(*Nisibis 16:1–4*)

In another hymn Ephrem introduces a further mirror analogy.
Now it is prayer that is the mirror: if this mirror is polished and
rightly directed, then it will reflect Christ's beauty. Such prayer
will be indeed theophanic, revealing something of the Godhead.
But wrongly directed, the mirror of prayer can also reflect the
ugliness of Satan:

Let our prayer be a mirror, Lord, placed before Your
    face;
then Your fair beauty will be imprinted on its luminous
    surface.
O Lord, let not the Evil One, who is ugly, gaze on it,
lest his ugliness be impressed upon it.

The mirror conceives the image of everyone who en-
    counters it.
Let not all sorts of thoughts be imprinted on our prayer;
Let the movements of Your face, Lord, settle upon it,
so that, like a mirror, it may be filled with Your beauty.

(*Church 29:9–10*)

But it is above all the Scriptures, and in particular the Gospels, which Ephrem delights to describe as a mirror. They are of course a polished mirror, always potentially capable of reflecting divine reality. But that does not mean that everyone can see this reality there: in order to see the reflection of Truth in the mirror of the Scriptures the eye of the beholder *also* needs, as we have already seen, to be clear and luminous:

> The Scriptures are placed there like a mirror:
> he whose eye is luminous beholds there the image of reality.
>
> (*Faith* 67:8)

One of Ephrem's most developed uses of mirror imagery is to be found in his letter to Publius, which takes the form of an extended meditation on judgement. In the course of this we learn that, not only does the 'polished mirror of the holy Gospel of your Lord' reflect the truth about divine reality, it also reflects the truth about the beholder, showing up whatever moral ugliness may be there:

> You do well not to let drop from your hands the polished mirror of the holy Gospel of your Lord, for it provides the likeness of everyone who looks into it, and it shows the resemblance of all who peer into it. And while it preserves its own nature and undergoes no change, having no spots and being quite free from any dirt, yet when coloured objects are put in front of it, it changes its aspect, though itself undergoes no change: when white objects are put in front of it, it turns white; when black ones, it takes on their hue; when red, it becomes red like them; and with beautiful objects, it reflects their beauty; with ugly, it becomes unsightly like them. It depicts in itself every limb of the body: it rebukes the defects of the ugly, so that they may remedy themselves, and remove the grime from their faces. To the beautiful it declares that they should be careful of their beauty, that it does not become spotted with dirt, but rather, they should add to their natural created beauty with adornments of their

own /hboxchoosing. Though dumb, the mirror speaks: in its silence, it cries out; although you might think it was a dead object, it makes its proclamation. Though still, it dances about; though it has no body, its womb is spacious, and in those hidden chambers within it every limb is depicted.All kinds of shapes are featured in the fraction of a moment, they are created within it with a speed that is imperceptible.

For this mirror is a figure of the holy preaching of the outward Gospel. Within itself is depicted the beauty of the beautiful who look into it, and again in it the defects of the ugly who despise it are rebuked. And just as this natural mirror is but a figure of the Gospel, so too the Gospel is but a figure of the beauty that is above which does not fade and at which all the sins of the created world are rebuked. For in it reward is given to all who have kept their beauty from being defiled with mud. For to everyone who peers into this mirror his sins are visible, and everyone who considers it, sees there the lot which is reserved for him, whether good or bad. There the kingdom of heaven is depicted, visible to those who have a luminous eye; there the lofty ranks of the good are to be seen on high, there the raised ranks of the intermediate can be distinguished, and there the low ranks of the wicked are marked out. There the fair places, prepared for those who are worthy of them, can be recognized, there Paradise is visible, joyous with its flowers. In that mirror Gehenna,[5] too, is visible, all fiery, ready for those who deserve to live there . . .

(*Letter to Publius 1–2*)

So far we have been concerned mainly with the preconditions, as Ephrem sees them, that are essential if someone is going to be able, in the first place to recognize God's types and symbols in Scripture and Nature, and then to read them correctly, making use of them as the ladder by which to make the ascent to spiritual knowledge.

Faith is the 'key' by which the door to the Kingdom of God can be opened, and faith is the initial 'offering' to God that needs to be made before any progress in knowledge of God becomes practicable:

> To You, Lord, do I offer my faith as an offering.
> I have offered it all naked, without any good deeds;
> it belongs to You, Lord, so let it be enriched by You,
> then I, for my part, who am so needy, will be enriched
>   by it.
>
> A merchant offers a pearl to a king,
> he receives it all naked, but he enhances it:
> the king enhances it by placing it on his crown
> —so how much more, Lord, will my faith be enhanced
>   in You?
>
> (*Faith 16:6–7*)

But how is further progress made? Once faith has been 'born', it requires nourishment in order to grow, and this nourishment is provided above all by praise, itself an outgrowth of the sense of wonder. Praise of the Creator, in Ephrem's eyes, is nothing less than the fulfilment of the intended role of created beings, whether spiritual beings such as the angels and seraphim, or the physical world around us. For rational human beings, endowed with free will, the choice *not* to praise God is a choice for death: 'I will give praise during my lifetime, and will not be a dead man among the living' (*Nisibis 50:1*, quoted in full in Chapter Two). It is praise which actually causes spiritual growth:

> I stood in fear, having become aware of You;
> I grew because I magnified You.
> Whereas You do not thereby grow,
> the person who increases praise of Your Majesty
> grows in You a great deal.
>
> (*Faith 32:5*)

And elsewhere Ephrem explains

Praises do not make God any the greater
—it is our mouths that are thereby exalted.

(Nicomedia 3:191–2)

Praise, as a response, starts out as vocal praise, but the more refined and purified it becomes, the more it takes on the character of the silent praise of the angelic beings *(Faith 4:1)*—appropriately enough seeing that it is as angelic beings that those who receive the 'bread of angels' in the Eucharist are in the process of being recreated *(Faith 10:9)*. There is thus a twofold movement from the silence of ingratitude to vocal praises, and then on to a different sort of silence, the silence of silent praise. This movement of praise from sound to silence is seen by Ephrem as a counterpart to the movement of God from the Silence of His ineffable Being to the divine Utterance, the Word.

Whereas the divine descent can be described as being increasingly kataphatic, the human ascent needs correspondingly to be increasingly apophatic.

SYMBOLS PERCEIVED

The vision of the luminous eye of faith needs to be enhanced by praise, otherwise faith remains like a chick unable to break out of its shell:

A chick not yet fully formed
in its weakness cannot break its shell;
so faith, held in silence,
is likewise weak. O perfect it, You who perfect all
    things.

(Faith 18:1)

Like the young bird of Ephrem's analogy in this hymn, faith must take wing if it is to grow up:

A bird grows up in three stages,
from womb to egg, then to the nest where it sings;
and once it is fully grown it flies in the air,
opening its wings in the symbol of the Cross.

(Faith 18:2)

The more the praise, the more the inner eye beholds, thus giving continuous reason for further praise. What sort of things does this 'luminous eye' behold? It is an infinitely exciting world, where the symbols, types and analogies latent in both Nature and the Scriptural text gradually become more and more perceptible. In the hymn whose opening has just been quoted it is the symbols of the Cross that Ephrem finds all around him—in the bird's opened wings, in the oars of a boat, in one's outstretched arms as one puts on a shirt. Here, in order to get some glimpse of the riches which Ephrem's own luminous eye discovers in 'the treasure store of symbols', we shall concentrate on one single area, centered round a single biblical verse. Ephrem exclaims in the response to one of the Paschal hymns:

> Praise to the Son, the Lord of symbols,
> who has fulfilled all kinds of symbols at His
>   Crucifixion.

> *(Unleavened Bread 3)*

The Crucifixion is not surprisingly one of the main focal points towards which symbols and types converge. Within the Gospel narrative there is one verse in particular which Syriac writers, from Ephrem on, see as being of central importance, offering a meeting point between past and future, looking back to the Genesis narrative of the Fall and the Exodus narrative (the rock in the Wilderness) and forwards to the sacramental life of the church. The verse is of course John 19:34: 'One of the soldiers pierced Jesus' side with a lance, and at once there came forth blood and water'.[6]

The verse provides three main starting points for typological exegesis: the side, the lance, and the issuing forth of blood and water. The side looks back to Adam's side, whence Eve was extracted (Genesis 2:22), the lance likewise looks back to the cherub's sword that guarded paradise after the expulsion of Adam and Eve (Gen. 3:24), while the issue of blood and water looks forward to the Mysteries of the Church, the Eucharist and Baptism.

Christ's Side and Adam's Side

This is an aspect on which Ephrem only touches explicitly

on rare occasions, and most notably in the *Commentary on the Diatessaron* (21:11), where he contrasts Eve who issued from the First Adam's rib with the Church which issues from the Second Adam's side:

> There came forth blood and water: that is, His Church, built on His side. Just as in the case of Adam, his wife was taken from his side, Adam's wife being his 'rib', so our Lord's blood is His Church. From Adam's rib came death, from our Lord's rib, life.

The Cherub's Sword and the Lance

This is the typological pair in which Ephrem shows most interest. The lance which pierced Christ's side effectively removes the cherub's sword that guarded Paradise. Often Ephrem uses the same word for both weapons, as in the following passage:

> Happy are you, living wood of the Cross,
> for you proved to be a hidden sword to Death;
> for with that sword which smote Him
> the Son slew Death, when He Himself was struck
>   by it.
> The sword that pierced Christ removed the sword
>   guarding Paradise;
> His forgiveness tore up our document of debt*   *Col. 2:14
>   (*Crucifixion 9:2*)

The piercing of Christ's side thus makes it possible for humanity to reenter Paradise:

> Blessed is the Merciful One who saw the sword
> beside Paradise, barring the way
> to the Tree of Life. He came and took Himself
> a body which was wounded

so that, by the opening of His side
He might open up the way to Paradise.

(*Nativity 8:4*)

Why the piercing of Christ's side should bring this about becomes evident when we turn to the third aspect.

The Issue of Blood and Water from the Pierced Side

We have already seen how, in the Commentary on the Diatessaron, Ephrem contrasted Eve's birth from Adam's side with the Church's birth from Christ's side. Just before the excerpt quoted, Ephrem indicates that by 'the Church' he specifically means the Mysteries or Sacraments:

Therefore there came forth the Blood by which He redeemed us from slavery; and water, so that everyone who approaches the Blood that gives him freedom should wash off that evil slavery to which he had been subjected.

(*Commentary on the Diatessaron 21:11*)

It is in the Eucharistic hymns preserved in Armenian that the sacramental interpretation—already clearly implicit in the passage just quoted—is most obviously found; thus, for the water representing baptism we have:

From the Wood on Golgotha
a fountain of life flowed forth for the Gentiles;

(*Armenian Hymns 49:8*)[7]

and for the blood we have a couple of starkly realistic passages:

Let us consume in holy fashion that Body
which the People pierced with their nails;
let us drink, as the Medicine of Life,
the Blood which flows from His side.

(*Armenian Hymns 48*: lines 1–4)

And (in the context of the Eucharistic Cup)

> Let us look with the hidden eye
>   and see Him hanging from the Tree;
> let our eyes behold the Blood
>   that flowed from His side.
>
> *(Armenian Hymns, 49:4)*

But it is not solely for the benefit of the 'Church of the Peoples', or Gentiles, that the blood and water flow:

> They transfixed You with nails
> —but You turned these into medicaments for their dis-
>   eases;
> they pierced You with the sword, and there sprung
>   forth water
> —for the wiping away of their sins:
> there came forth water, and blood too,
> so that they might stand in awe
> and wash their hands from Your blood.
> The Slain One provided from His own blood
> the water wherewith His slayers might wash clean
> and themselves find life.
>
> *(Virginity 30:10)*

The blood and water from Christ's side are for the benefit of all humanity, and so Ephrem can describe the piercing as providing baptism for Adam himself, so that he can return to Paradise:

> There came forth from Christ water:
> Adam washed, revived, and returned to Paradise.
>
> *(Nisibis 39:7)*

There are other biblical passages, too, with which Ephrem links John 19:34, either explicitly or implicitly by way of verbal allusion. Among the former we may note the sword of Phinehas (Numbers 25:7–8; *Nisibis 39*) and the Rock in the Wilderness (Exodus 17:6, Numbers 20:11 and 1 Corinthians 10:4, where this 'spiritual rock' is identified as Christ):[8]

> The fact that Paul calls that rock Christ is because the
> side of our Lord was torn open and there gushed forth

from it blood and water, blood for propitiation, and for
all peoples to drink.
     (*Commentary on the Pauline Epistles*, p.68 = p.66)

Thus the pierced side of John 19:34 is intimately associated, in
Ephrem's inner eye, with another exceedingly rich 'fountain of
symbols', which we cannot begin to explore here.

Later poets were to draw out yet further typological associations
for the verse, and Jacob of Serugh (who died in 521) in particular
introduces bridal imagery into the episode in a highly dramatic
and imaginative way.[9]

Since we have been examining Ephrem's handling of this particular verse, John 19:34, in an analytical way, it will be appropriate
to remind ourselves at the conclusion that the whole aim of this
type of interpretation is not any historical or scientific knowledge,
but the furtherance of spiritual awareness, a reciprocation, no less,
of divine love. Perhaps nowhere in Ephrem's writings can we see
this more clearly than in the following passage of lyrical beauty
from his *Commentary on the Diatessaron (21:10)*, where he addresses
Christ directly:

> I ran to all Your limbs, and from them I received every
> kind of gift. Through the side pierced with the sword
> I entered the garden fenced in by the sword. Let us
> enter in through that side which was pierced, since we
> were stripped naked by the counsel of the rib that was
> extracted. The fire that burnt in Adam, burnt him in
> that rib of his; for this reason the side of the Second
> Adam has been pierced, and from it comes forth a flow
> of water to quench the fire of the First Adam.[10]

5

THE ROBE OF GLORY

IN ONE OF THE HYMNS on the Nativity Saint Ephrem writes concerning the Incarnation and its effects in the following terms:

> All these changes did the Merciful One make,
> stripping off glory and putting on a body;
> for He had devised a way to reclothe Adam
> in that glory which Adam had stripped off.
> Christ was wrapped in swaddling clothes,
> corresponding to Adam's leaves,
> Christ put on clothes, instead of Adam's skins;
> He was baptized for Adam's sin,
> His body was embalmed for Adam's death,
> He rose and raised up Adam in his glory.
> Blessed is He who descended, put Adam on and ascended!
>
> *(Nativity 23:13)*

Here, within the space of a single stanza Ephrem has covered the entire span of salvation history, employing his favourite imagery of 'putting on' and 'taking off' clothing. At the Fall Adam was stripped of glory—his 'robe of glory', but this effect of the Fall is reversed by the Divine Word 'stripping off His own glory' and 'putting on a body', or, as the last line of the stanza has it, when

'He put on Adam', that is, humanity, and so raised humanity to its original state, clothed in the 'robe of glory'.

By means of this clothing imagery Ephrem succeeds in providing his readers with a splendidly cohesive picture of the entire range of salvation history, from Creation to the Fall, through the Incarnation, to the Sacraments, or Mysteries, of Baptism and the Eucharist, and on to the Final Resurrection. The continuum is provided above all by the image of the 'robe of glory' (or 'robe of praise', as it could also be translated), a robe which Ephrem sometimes also calls the 'robe of light'.

THE PRIMORDIAL ROBE

It is worth reflecting briefly on the origins of this idea of the 'robe of glory or light' in which Adam and Eve were originally clothed.[1] It by no means originates with Ephrem, and indeed it was extremely popular in some circles outside Christianity altogether, among the Mandaeans and Manichaeans. Ephrem, and Syriac Christianity in general, evidently inherited this image of the primordial 'robe of light' or 'glory' from Jewish interpretations of Genesis 3:21, 'And the Lord God made for Adam and his wife garments of skin, and He clothed them'. These interpretations were circulating around the turn of the Christian era.

Ancient exegetes asked themselves two quite different questions in connection with this verse. What were these garments? And to what time does the verse refer—after the Fall (as is usually understood by modern commentators), or might it be before the Fall? If the verse referred to before the Fall, then it would be a summarizing statement: 'Now God had made these garments for them', that is, before the Fall. There is evidence that such an interpretation was at one time quite widespread.

Going back to the first question, 'what were these 'garments of skin'?', we encounter a great variety of different answers in both Jewish and Christian writers, but for our purpose two interpretations found in Jewish sources are of significance in connection with this theme of the primordial 'robe of glory'.

Firstly, if we look at the Targum tradition, we discover at Genesis 3:21, not the 'garments of skin', as the Hebrew text has it, but

'clothing of glory', very close to the phrase employed by Ephrem
and other Syriac writers. Then secondly, if we turn to the Jewish
Midrash Rabba on Genesis, we learn that the famous first-century
Rabbi Meir was reputed to have possessed a Hebrew manuscript
of the Pentateuch which read in this verse, Gen. 3:21, not 'garments of skin', but 'garments of light' (there is only a single letter's
difference in Hebrew).

We can be certain that the idea of a primordial 'robe of glory'
has its origin in Jewish speculation concerning Genesis 3:21; it will
have reached Christian (and other) circles by way of the extensive
apocryphal literature, now for the most part lost, that grew up
around the figures of Adam and Eve in the early centuries of the
Christian era.

Ephrem frequently alludes to the primordial clothing of glory;
in his Commentary on Genesis he refers to it in particular in
connection with Genesis 2:25, 'the two of them were naked, but
they were not ashamed'. Here Ephrem comments:

> It was because of the glory in which they were wrapped
> that they were not ashamed. Once this glory had been
> taken away from them, after the transgression of the
> commandment, they were ashamed, because they had
> been stripped of the glory. Thereupon the two of them
> rushed to the fig leaves in order to cover, not so much
> their bodies, as their shameful members.
>
> (*Comm. Gen. 2:14*)

THE RECOVERY OF THE ROBE

The entire purpose of the Incarnation is to reclothe Adam, that
is humanity, in this lost 'robe of glory':

> Christ came to find Adam who had gone astray,
> He came to return him to Eden in the garment of light.
>
> (*Virginity 16:9*)

And with specific reference to Eve:

> Eve looked to Christ, for great was the nakedness of
>   women,

and it was Christ who was able to reclothe them
in the glory they had stripped off, thus replacing the
leaves.

(Nativity 1:43)

The theme of the fig leaves (Genesis 3:7) is picked up by Ephrem
in the *Commentary on the Diatessaron (16:10)*:

When Adam sinned and was stripped of the glory in
which he had been clothed, he covered his nakedness
with fig leaves. Our Saviour came and underwent suffering in order to heal Adam's wounds and to provide a
garment of glory for his nakedness. He dried up the fig
tree (Matthew 21:20–21) in order to show that there
would no longer be any need for fig leaves to serve as
Adam's garment, since Adam had returned to his former glory, and so no longer had any need of leaves or
'garments of skin'.

Elsewhere he exclaims:

Blessed is He who had pity on Adam's leaves
and sent a robe of glory to cover his naked state.

(Fast 3:2)

As we have often had occasion to observe, 'to put on the body'
is Ephrem's favourite metaphor for the Incarnation, and it is in
order to bring out the continuity of salvation history that he often
extends the image to include specific reference to Adam:

Glory to You, who clothed Yourself in the body of
mortal Adam, thereby making it a fountain of life (*or*
salvation) for all mortals.

(Discourse on our Lord 9)

We should note how very close are the links, in Ephrem's mind,
between Adam, Christ and humanity in passages such as the following;

He put on Adam, and by him
Burst open Paradise at His entry.

(Heresies 26:6)

Through the Second Adam who entered Paradise

> everyone has entered it;
> for through the First Adam who left it,
> everyone had left it.
>
> (*Unleavened Bread 17:10*)

Likewise, just as God the Word 'puts on the body of Adam', so too Ephrem describes Him as 'putting on our body' (*Church 42*, refrain).

When meditating on 'the great wonder' of the Nativity, Ephrem introduces the theme of 'the robe of glory' into two different contexts. First, it is Christ's mother Mary who is the initial mortal to be reclothed in this robe. In the following excerpt it is Mary herself who is speaking in the first person:

> The Son of the Most High came and dwelt in me,
> and I became His mother.
> Just as I gave birth to Him
> —a further birth, so too did He give birth to me
> —a second birth: He put on His mother's robe
> —her body, while I put on His glory.
>
> (*Nativity 16:11*)

In this tightly packed stanza we can observe once more the pattern of reciprocity and complementarity which Ephrem so much likes to explore: Christ's first birth from the Father and His second birth from Mary are balanced chiastically here with Mary's physical birth and her second birth, in other words, her baptism which, as we shall see, Ephrem regards as already taking place while Christ is in her womb.

Mary's acquisition of the robe of glory is specifically contrasted with Eve's loss of it in another Nativity hymn:

> Eve in her virginity put on leaves of shame,
> but Your mother, Lord, in her virginity
> has put on a robe of glory
> that encompasses all people,

> while to Him who covers all
> she gives a body as a tiny garment.
>
> (*Nativity 17:4*)

Mary's robe of glory that encompasses all people brings us to the second context within the Nativity narrative where Ephrem introduces the imagery of the robe: this is in connection with the swaddling clothes with which the infant Christ is wrapped:

> In Bethlehem did king David put on fine linen,
> but David's Lord and Son
> hid His glory there in His swaddling clothes.
> These same swaddling clothes
> provided a robe of glory for humankind.
>
> (*Nativity 5:4*)

CHRIST'S BAPTISM AND CHRISTIAN BAPTISM

The next stage in the history of the robe of glory comes with Christ's baptism in the river Jordan. In the early Syriac Church this event was seen as the fountainhead of all Christian baptism: there Christ 'opens up baptism' (*Virginity 15:3*), and the Gospel narratives of Christ's own baptism are seen, not only as the public proclamation of His divine Sonship, but also as a manifestation to the human senses of the Trinity (*Faith 51:7*): the Father to the hearing, by means of the divine voice and proclamation, the Son to the touch, and the Spirit to the sight, in the bodily form of the dove. The trinitarian character of Christ's baptism is picked up for Ephrem in His subsequent instruction to the Apostles 'to baptize in the name of the Father, Son and Holy Spirit' (Matthew 28:19).

Ephrem looks at Christ's baptism from two somewhat different standpoints. On the one hand it is part of the process of the 'mingling in ' (as Ephrem liked to express it) of God with the human experience. Thus, the Word not only 'puts on a body', but He also 'puts on the waters of baptism' (*Nativity 12:2*). Elsewhere, playing on the double meaning of the Syriac verb *'mad*, meaning both 'to be baptized' and 'to dive', Ephrem describes Christ as

diving for the treasure that will give life and salvation to Adam's
children:

> Christ, though immortal by nature, clothed Himself in
>   a mortal body;
> He was baptized (*or* He dived down)—and raised up
>   from the water
> the treasure of salvation for the race of Adam.
>
> > (*Virginity 7:10*)

Ephrem's second standpoint shows a more specific concern to
associate Christ's baptism with Christian baptism. In a remarkable
hymn[2] on Christ in the river Jordan and in the womb of Mary
Ephrem links these two aspects: Christ's baptism in 'the womb'
of the Jordan looks back in time to His conception in Mary's
womb. Both wombs, Mary's and the Jordan's, by bearing Christ
the Light, are clothed with light from His presence within them;
Mary's womb thus becomes the source of her own baptism, the
Jordan's womb becomes the fountainhead of Christian baptism:

> The river in which Christ was baptized
> conceived Him again symbolically;
> the moist womb of the water
> conceived Him in purity,
> bore Him in chastity,
> made Him go up in glory.
>
> In the pure womb of the river
> you should recognize Mary, the daughter of humanity,
> who conceived having known no man,
> who gave birth without intercourse,
> who brought up, through a gift,
> the Lord of that gift.
>
> As the Daystar in the river,
> the Bright One in the tomb,
> He shone forth on the mountain top
> and gave brightness too in the womb;

> He dazzled as He went up from the river,
> gave illumination at His ascent.
>
> The brightness which Moses put on
> was wrapped on him from without,
> whereas the river in which Christ was baptized
> was clothed in light from within;
> so too did Mary's body, in which He resided,
> gleam from within.
>
> *(Church 36:3–6)*

We already encountered a little earlier the idea that Mary 'put on the robe of glory', at her second—baptismal—birth, from Christ's presence in her womb. How are we to understand this anticipation of baptism, before Christ had even 'opened up' baptism in the Jordan? The same sort of problem might be seen to apply to the early Syriac emphasis on Christ's baptism in the Jordan as the source of Christian baptism, apparently ignoring the role of His death and resurrection. From the point of view of linear historical time all this is indeed bizarre and illogical, but Ephrem's thought clearly makes use here of the concept of sacred time: the total effect of the Incarnation is operative at any single point along its main 'staging posts' (as Ephrem often calls them)[3], that is to say, Mary's womb, the 'womb' of the Jordan, and the 'womb' of Sheol. Thus what is still to be effected by Christ in historical time by His death and resurrection can be anticipated in sacred time already while He is still in the womb, or at His baptism in the Jordan.

In other passages Ephrem may look specifically forward from Christ's baptism to Christian baptism: thus in the Commentary on the Diatessaron (4:3) the descent of the Spirit at Christ's baptism indicated that the Spirit is given by baptism. In the Discourse on our Lord (55) Ephrem even speaks of 'the robe of the Spirit':

> John whitened the stains of sins with ordinary water,
> so that bodies might be rendered suitable for the robe
> of the Spirit that is given through our Lord. Because
> the Spirit was with the Son, the Son came to John in

order to receive baptism from him, so that He might mix with the visible water the Spirit who cannot be seen, so that those whose bodies perceive the wetness of the water might perceive in their minds the gift of the Spirit.

Or the same idea may be put in a much more succinct form:

Our body was Your clothing, Your Spirit was our robe.
(*Nativity 22:39*)

Later writers, especially Jacob of Serugh, will apply the imagery of the robe of glory more explicitly to Christ's baptism; thus Jacob writes 'Christ came to baptism, He went down and placed in the baptismal water the robe of glory, to be there for Adam, who had lost it'.[4]

Christ's baptism, and the sanctification of the Jordan waters provide the occasion for the recovery of the lost robe of glory in Christian baptism. Already in Saint Paul we have clothing imagery of 'putting on Christ' at baptism, and this is directly reflected in one of the Hymns against Heresies (17:5):

Body and soul together exalt You,
for they have been baptized in You
and have put You on.

The imagery is frequent in the Epiphany hymns attributed to Ephrem (but which are probably somewhat later); there we have the robe of glory once again directly introduced:

O children of the baptismal font,
babes who without spot have put on Fire and Spirit,
preserve the glorious robe
that you have put on from the water.

Whosoever puts on the robe of glory
from the water and the Spirit,
will destroy with its burning
the thorny growth of his sins.

(*Epiphany 4:19–20*)

In another of this group of hymns Adam's recovery of the robe of glory is specifically connected with baptism; once again Adam is both individual and generic here:

> In baptism did Adam find
> that glory which had been his among the trees of Paradise;
> he went down and took it from the water,
> put it on, went up and was held in honour in it.
>
> > (*Epiphany 12:1*)

In the former of these Epiphany hymns there are two features which are also characteristic of the genuine hymns of Ephrem: the close association between Fire and Spirit, and the idea of 'preserving' the robe of glory.

In the Gospels Jesus already promises to baptize with Fire and Spirit, and from the second century onwards a tradition grew up that at Jesus' baptism fire and/or light appeared on the Jordan.[5] In Syriac tradition the fire plays a very important role in the context of baptism, and in Ephrem the theme will be linked with his image of the Trinity as Sun, Light and Heat, an analogy which he develops in two of the Hymns on Faith (40 and 73). In a Eucharistic hymn, to which we shall be returning in the next chapter, Christ's presence in Mary's womb, in the Jordan and in the consecrated Host, is likewise described as Fire:

> See, Fire and Spirit in the womb that bore You,
> see, Fire and Spirit in the river in which You were baptized.
> Fire and Spirit in our Baptism,
> in the Bread and the Cup, Fire and Holy Spirit.
>
> > (*Faith 10:17*)

THE WEDDING GARMENT

When the newly baptized are told to 'preserve' their recently acquired 'robe of glory', there lies behind this an allusion to the parable of the wedding in Matthew 22:1–14, where the guest who turns up at the wedding feast without his wedding garment is thrown out. From later writers we learn explicitly that the wedding garment is none other than 'the robe of glory', acquired at baptism, which must be kept unspotted for the eschatological wedding feast: it is *not* the case that the wedding guest never had a wedding garment; rather, he had been given one—at baptism—but he had lost or soiled it.

Such an interpretation of the parable of Matthew 22 was clearly already current in the Syriac Church by Ephrem's time,[6] for Ephrem gives an intriguing twist to the imagery:

> The First-born wrapped Himself in a body
> as a veil to hide His glory.
> The immortal Bridegroom shines out in that robe:
> let the guests in their clothing resemble Him in His.
> Let your bodies—which are your clothing—
> shine out, for they bound in fetters
> that man whose body was stained.
> Lord, do You whiten my stains at Your banquet with
> Your radiance.

> (*Nisibis 43:21*)

Here Ephrem, with deliberate paradox, identifies the wedding garment of the parable, not with the baptismal robe of glory (as his readers might have expected), but with the actual bodies of the wedding guests, which are to correspond to the radiance and glory of Christ's body, that is, the garment that the Heavenly Bridegroom Himself put on.

The parable of the wedding guest in Matthew 22 can also serve to illustrate the tension between the baptismal and eschatological roles of the robe of glory. The distribution of the wedding garments, the baptismal robes of glory, is envisaged as taking place in historical time, at baptism, while the actual wedding feast belongs to sacred time, to the eschaton, when the righteous, those who have 'preserved' their wedding garments spotless, will fully realize the existence of their robes of glory.

The concept of an eschatological robe of glory is already found in Judaism of the inter-testamental period, and it is fully familiar to Ephrem. Thus, in the Paradise Hymns he writes:

> Among the saints none is naked,
> for they have put on glory;
> nor is there any clad in fig leaves,
> or standing in shame,
> for they have found, through our Lord,
> the robe that belonged to Adam and Eve.
>
> *(Paradise 6:9)*

The same tension between the robe of glory put on 'now' at baptism, and its wearing at the eschatological banquet is to be found in many other related contexts of Ephrem's thought: thus the Church herself represents both Paradise on earth and the eschatological Paradise (in Ephrem's thought Paradise and the Kingdom are more or less synonymous). Similarly Christ Himself represents the Tree of Life, of whose fruits the baptized already partake in this life at the Eucharist. Eschatological Paradise, with the robe of glory and the Tree of Life, is thus potentially present already in historical time, but it will only be fully realized at the eschaton, outside historical time. For Ephrem the sacramental life, fully lived, is the anticipation of the eschatological Paradise here on earth: how far this eschatological Paradise can be realized and experienced by the Christian will depend on each individual's openness to the sense of wonder, and his or her possession of the luminous inner eye of faith.

In the Commentary on the Diatessaron Ephrem makes use of Saint Paul's image of 'the pledge' to illustrate the relationship between Paradise experienced potentially now, and fully at the eschaton:

> Again we would say 'If Adam died because of sin, He who removed sin had to take away death too'. But just as Adam was told 'The day you eat of the forbidden tree, you shall die', but in fact he did not die; but rather he received a pledge of his death in the form of being stripped naked of the glory and his expulsion from Paradise, after which he was daily pondering on death. It is exactly the same with life in Christ: we have eaten His Body in place of the fruit of the Tree, and

His altar has taken the place of the Garden of Eden for us; the curse has been washed away by His innocent blood, and in the hope of resurrection we await the life that is to come, and indeed we already walk in this new life, in that we already have a pledge of it.

(*Commentary on the Diatessaron 21:25*)

6

THE MEDICINE OF LIFE[1]

CHRIST IS THE 'MEDICINE OF LIFE which flew down from on high' (*Discourse 3*). Previously 'Moses had hidden the symbol of Christ as a Medicine of Life in the unleavened bread' (*Unleavened Bread 18:15*), and Ruth had already recognized the hidden presence of the Medicine of Life in Jesus' ancestor Boaz (*Nativity 1:13*). At the Last Supper 'the Lifegiver of all blessed the food and it became the Medicine of Life for those who ate it' (*Unleavened Bread 14:16*), and at the descent into the underworld Ephrem writes:

> Let Eve today rejoice in Sheol,
> for her daughter's Son
> has come down as the Medicine of Life
> to revive His mother's mother.
>
> (*Nativity 13:2*)

It is above all Christ's hidden presence in the Eucharistic Bread and Cup that is for Ephrem the Medicine of Life:

> The Grape of Mercy was pressed
> and gave the Medicine of Life to the Peoples.
>
> (*Virginity 31:3*)
> Our Lord baptized humankind with the Holy Spirit,
> He nourished it with the Medicine of Life.
>
> (*Nisibis 46:8*)

In the present chapter we shall be looking at something of the part that the Eucharist plays in the life of the Church. It is a subject on which Ephrem has a great deal to say and so our picture will of necessity only be a very selective one.

Ephrem envisages daily Communion, and to this he gives paradisiacal overtones:

> The assembly of the saints
>   bears resemblance to Paradise:
> in it, each day, is plucked the fruit
> of Him who gives life to all.

(Paradise 6:8)

Entry into the Church at baptism is, as we have seen, a re-entry into Paradise, but the eschatological Paradise which is anticipated by the Church is far more glorious than the primordial one, as we learn from one of Ephrem's Eucharistic hymns preserved only in Armenian (49:9–11); here Ephrem begins by contrasting the cherub's sword excluding Adam from Paradise with Christ's pierced side:

> With the blade of the sword of the cherub
>   was the path to the Tree of Life shut off,
> but to the Peoples the Lord of that Tree
>   has given Himself as food.
>
> Whereas Eden's other trees were provided
>   for the former Adam to eat,
> for us the very Planter of the Garden
>   has become the food for our souls.
>
> Whereas we had left that Garden
>   along with Adam when he left it behind,
> now that the sword has been removed by the lance
>   we may return there.

We can observe once again how closely Ephrem associates Adam's experience with our experience: 'we left that Garden along with Adam when he left it behind'. This solidarity of humanity with Adam also comes out prominently in another passage,

where, however, our solidarity with Adam is juxtaposed with the
solidarity of Christ, the Second Adam, with us; in this hymn
Ephrem is combining the theme of the Eucharist as re-entry into
Paradise with certain features from the Exodus narrative:

> Earthly creatures consumed the heavenly Manna
> —and they became dust on the earth, because of their
>   sins.
>
> The spiritual Bread of the Eucharist
> makes light and causes to fly:
> the Peoples have been wafted up
> and have settled in Paradise.
>
> Through the Second Adam who entered Paradise
> everyone has entered it,
> for through the First Adam who left it
> everyone left it.
>
> By means of the Spiritual Bread
> everyone becomes
> an eagle who reaches
> as far as Paradise.
>
> Whoever eats the Living Bread of the Son
> flies to meet Him in the very clouds.
>
> (*Unleavened Bread 17:8–12*)

Earlier in this hymn Ephrem is primarily concerned with the Unleavened Bread of the Passover as a 'symbol of the Bread of Life'
(17:5); with Christ reality or 'truth' takes over from symbol, the
Bread of Life takes the place of the Unleavened Bread; the True
Lamb takes the place of the passover lamb. This occurs for Ephrem
at the Last Supper, which he takes to be the Passover meal (following the account of Luke and the other synoptic Gospels): at the
Last Supper Christ 'sacrificed Himself', prior to His actual death.[2]
This is described in very realistic terms in one of the Armenian
hymns:

It was the very same Christ in the Upper Room
    who gave and was distributed to all.
Even though the People slew Him,
    He had previously slain Himself with His own hand.

It was one slain by His own hands
    that the crazed ones crucified on Golgotha,
had He not slain Himself in symbol,
    they would not have slain Him in actual fact.
                          (*Armenian hymns 48*, lines 41–48)

In a hymn where he addresses the Upper Room itself Ephrem
further meditates on these paradoxes; after a stanza where he associates the footwashing with baptism, he continues:

Blessed are you, O Upper Room, so small
    in comparison to the entirety of creation,
yet what took place in you
    now fills all creation—which is even too small for it.
Blessed is your abode, for in it was broken
    that Bread which issues from the blessed Wheat
    Sheaf,
and in you was trodden out
    the Cluster of Grapes that came from Mary
to become the Cup of Salvation.

Blessed are you, O Upper Room,
    no man has ever seen
nor ever shall see, what you beheld:
    Our Lord became at once
True Altar, Priest, Bread, and Cup of Salvation.
    In His own person He could fulfil all these roles,
none other was capable of this:
    Whole Offering and Lamb, Sacrifice and Sacrificer,
Priest and the One destined to be consumed.
                          (*Crucifixion 3:9–10*)

The tension between the conflicting Passion chronologies of
the Synoptic Gospels and Saint John is preserved by Ephrem,

but instead of treating them as contradictory, he characteristically transforms apparent contradiction into a creative equilibrium. It is not a case of either/or, as historical exegesis would require: from Ephrem's theological standpoint, both accounts are correct.

Later in this chapter we shall see how Ephrem makes use of the chronology of Passover to draw out the parallelism which he sees between the Eucharist and the Incarnation. But before we turn to this topic (important for the understanding of the structure of Ephrem's thinking), we should turn our attention to two particular images of the Eucharist which are of significance to Ephrem. Appropriately, one is from Scripture, and the other from Nature, God's two witnesses.

THE COAL OF FIRE

Ephrem employs the term 'Coal of Fire', derived from the vision in the temple of the prophet Isaiah (Isaiah 6:6), with reference to both Christ Himself[3] and to the Eucharist:

> The Coal of Fire that came to burn away thorns and thistles (Genesis 3:18) dwelt in a womb, refining and sanctifying that place of pangs and curses (Genesis 3:16).
>
> (*Commentary on the Diatessaron 1:5*)

Appropriately enough Ephrem picks up the image in a delightful way when he describes the presentation of Christ in the Temple (Luke 2:38):

> The prophetess Anna embraced Him
> and put her mouth to His lips.
> The Spirit rested on her lips, as on Isaiah's;
> his mouth was silent, but the Coal of Fire
> opened up his mouth by touching his lips.
> Anna's mouth too became fervent with the Spirit (*or*
>   breath) from His mouth
> and she sang to Him: 'O royal Son, o lowly Son,
> You listen in stillness, You see, but are hidden,
> You know but are unknown;
> O God and Human, praise to Your Name'.
>
> (*Nativity 6:13–14*)

In Isaiah's vision the coal of fire is held by the seraph in tongs, and it merely touches Isaiah's lips. The fact that Christians actually hold and consume Christ the new Coal of Fire is for Ephrem a source of utter astonishment:

> The seraph could not touch the coal of fire with his
>   fingers,
> and the coal merely touched Isaiah's mouth:
> the seraph did not hold it, Isaiah did not consume it,
> but our Lord has allowed us to do both.
>
> (*Faith 10:10*)

For Ephrem the coal of fire in Isaiah 6 is but a specific example of the way in which the divinity can be spoken of as fire; earlier in the same hymn he writes:

> In Your Bread, Lord, there is hidden the Spirit who is
>   not consumed,
> in Your Wine there dwells the Fire that is not drunk:
> the Spirit is in Your Bread, the Fire in Your Wine,
> a manifest wonder, that our lips have received.
>
> (*Faith 10:8*)

It is the descent of the Spirit as Fire that effects the consecration of the Bread and Wine. The idea of the descent of fire in this context derives from a number of Old Testament passages where the descent of fire upon a sacrifice denotes the divine acceptance of that sacrifice (e.g. 2 Chronicles 7:1, Solomon's dedication of the Temple). In this tenth hymn on Faith, Ephrem specifically refers to Elijah's sacrifice on mount Carmel (1 Kings 18:38), also consumed by the descent of divine fire:

> Fire descended and consumed Elijah's sacrifices;
> the Fire of Mercy has become a living sacrifice for us:
> fire consumed Elijah's oblation,
> but we, Lord, have consumed Your Fire in Your obla-
>   tion.

This divine fire is to be held in the greatest awe, for it can be destructive in the case of sinners, just as much as life-giving, as

Ephrem warns in the previous stanza where he draws attention to one particular Old Testament example where this happened:

> Fire descended in wrath and consumed the sinners
>   (Genesis 19:24).
> The Fire of Mercy has now descended and dwelt in
>   the Bread:
> instead of that fire which consumed mankind,
> we have consumed Fire in the Bread—and we have
>   come to life.

But in consuming this new Fire there is danger too, for it can lead to judgement as well as to sanctification; echoing Saint Paul's words in I Corinthians 11:29, Ephrem says:

> For he who receives that Medicine of Life unworthily
>   takes judgement upon himself:
> it is a matter for wonder that such a person
>   has, in reverse, gained death by means of Life.
>   (*Armenian hymns* 47, lines 13–14)

The aim of consuming this divine Fire is of course the opposite: it effects sanctification, 'it gives perfection to all' (*Unleavened Bread 1:10*):

> When the Lord came down to earth to mortal beings
>   He created them again, a new creation, like the an-
>   gels,
> mingling within them Fire and Spirit,
>   so that in a hidden manner they too might be of
>   Fire and Spirit.
>   (*Faith 10:9*)

The process of assimilation to fire and spirit—the angelic state—is in fact a growing into conformity with Christ. Ephrem can speak of this assimilation in boldly vivid terms:

> Christ's Body has newly been mingled with our bodies,
> His Blood too has been poured out into our veins,
> His voice is in our ears,
> His brightness in our eyes.

In His compassion the whole of Him has been mingled
in with the whole of us.

(*Virginity 37:2*)

THE PEARL

Ephrem's five poems on the Pearl, coming near the end of the
hymn cycle on Faith, are among his most famous:

One day, my brethren, I took a pearl into my hands;
in it I beheld symbols which told of the Kingdom,
images and figures of God's majesty.
It became a fountain from which I drank the mysteries
of the Son.

(*Faith 81:1*)

As Ephrem meditatively turns over the pearl it suggests to his fertile
mind many different symbols: the Kingdom is of course already
found in the Gospels (Matthew 13:45), but to this Ephrem adds
Truth, Faith, the Church, Mary, Virginity, but above all Christ
Himself and His Body.

In the luminosity of the pearl I saw the
Luminous One*   *Shaphya
who cannot be perturbed; in its purity
is a wonderful symbol—the Body of our Lord,
wholly unsullied.

(*Faith 81:3*)

A few stanzas later eucharistic symbolism will provide one of the
several resonances:

Like the Manna which of its own sufficed
to fill the People, in place of other foods,
thanks to its tastiness, so too has the Pearl
filled me, replacing books (*or* Scripture)
and the reading and commenting on them.

(*Faith 81:8*)

The pearl acts as a symbol of the Eucharistic Host more obviously in the last of the five hymns on the pearl. In the following

stanzas there is an elaborate play on the word *shliḥe*, which has several different meanings: it can mean 'stripped naked', which can either be in the sense of the pearl divers, or refer to those being baptized, stripped of their clothes at baptism; alternatively *shliḥe* can mean 'apostles', 'those sent'. In the present extract 'naked (pearl divers)' and 'apostles' are the two uppermost senses, and since both are intended I have sometimes resorted to double translation:

Men stripped bare dived down and drew you up,
o Pearl. It was not kings
who first presented you to humankind,
but men stripped, symbols of the apostles, poor Galilean
fishermen.

They could not approach you with their bodies clothed
so they came stripped, like little children;
they buried their bodies and descended to you.
You eagerly met them and you take refuge in them
because they loved you so.

The tongues of these poor men, the apostles,
proclaimed glad tidings of you before they opened their
bosoms
and brought out their new wealth to show it
amidst the merchants, placing you
in people's hands as the Medicine of Life.

                    (*Faith 85:6–8*)

In these poems on the pearl and the pearl divers there is also an undercurrent of another play on words, for the verb *'mad* means both 'to dive' and 'to be baptized'. The baptized as it were dive down into the baptismal font and bring up Christ the Pearl (the Syrian baptismal rite of course concludes with Communion).

It was widely thought in antiquity that the pearl came into existence when lightning struck the mussel in the sea. This birth through the conjunction of two disparate elements is seen by Ephrem as a symbol of Christ's birth in the flesh from the Holy

Spirit, the Fire, and from Mary, 'the watery flesh'. Christ is thus both the Eucharistic Pearl and the Pearl born of the Holy Spirit and Mary. It is to the parallelism between Incarnation and Eucharist that we now turn.

INCARNATION AND EPICLESIS

Ephrem expresses the close relationship between Incarnation and Eucharist in a number of different ways. In the tenth hymn on Faith, from which so many quotations have already been drawn, the parallelism is brought out through the common presence of the Divine Fire:

> See, Fire and Spirit are in the womb of her who bore
>   You;
> see, Fire and Spirit are in the river in which You were
>   baptized.
> Fire and Spirit are in our baptismal font,
> in the Bread and the Cup are Fire and Holy Spirit.
>
> *(Faith 10:17)*

It can also be indicated by clothing imagery: if the body is evil, as the Marcionites say, 'how could Christ have despised the body yet *put on* the Bread?', asks Ephrem (*Heresies 47:2*; quoted above, p. 37); since they are related, either both are evil or both are good. Elsewhere, just as Christ's human body is 'the garment of His divinity' (*Faith 19:2*), so too the Eucharistic Bread is another garment:

> Who will not be amazed at Your various garments?
> The body has hidden Your radiance—the awesome di-
>   vine nature;
> ordinary clothes hid the feeble human nature;
> the Bread has hidden the Fire that resides within it.
>
> *(Faith 19:3)*

The mystery that occurred at the moment of the Incarnation and the mystery that occurs at the epiclesis in the Eucharistic Liturgy are seen throughout all Syriac tradition as intimately connected.[4] It is well known that this applies to both East and

West Syrian developments in later centuries, but it is just as much a feature of Saint Ephrem's thought already in the fourth century. There are two further notable ways in which Ephrem draws attention to this structural relationship. One involves his understanding of the chronology of the Annunciation and conception, while the other involves his usage of particular terminology.

The date which we now associate with the Annunciation, March 25th, does not appear to have become at all prominent until the sixth century; it is obviously linked with the Feast of the Nativity on 25th December, a date which was certainly not yet known to Ephrem. In Syriac liturgical tradition, both East and West, it is with the Sundays immediately before the Nativity that the Annunciation (*Subbara*) is associated. In Ephrem's day, however, quite a different date for the Annunciation was known: 10th Nisan (April). How did this arise, and what is its significance to our present concern?

The date 10th Nisan for the Annunciation (and hence, conception) was arrived at by a clever piece of calculation, based on the data available in the Gospel narratives, combined with the assumption (historically incorrect) that Zechariah, the Baptist's father, was high priest.[5] Thus Ephrem, in his *Commentary on the Diatessaron* (1:14) speaks of Zechariah's vision as taking place, not by the altar of incense (Luke 1:11), but in the Holy of Holies. Since the Holy of Holies was only entered by the High Priest once a year, on the Day of Atonement, this now gave a fixed date, 10th Tishri I, for an event mentioned in the Infancy narrative of Saint Luke's Gospel. Turning to Luke 1:36, the Annunciation to Mary, we learn that this was six months after the angel's promise to Zechariah of a son, that is to say, six months after 10th of Tishri I, which provides 10th Nisan.

But why was 10th Nisan significant for Ephrem? Here is how he explains it in his *Commentary on Exodus* (12:2–3):

> The passover lamb is a symbol of our Lord who came to
> the womb on the tenth of Nisan. For, from the tenth of
> the seventh month (Tishri), when Zechariah was told
> about the birth of John, up to the first month (Nisan),

when the announcement was made to Mary by the angel, constitute six months. That was why the angel said to her 'This is the sixth month for her who had been called barren'. On the tenth of Nisan, therefore, when the passover lamb was confined (see Exodus 12:3), our Lord was conceived, and on the fourteenth, when it was slaughtered, He whom the lamb symbolized was crucified.

Thus Christ, 'the true Passover Lamb', enters Mary's womb on 10th Nisan, in conformity with the law of Exodus 12:3, and then (as we saw earlier in this chapter) 'sacrifices himself' as the Passover Lamb at the Last Supper. In this way, by means of the imagery of the passover lamb and the chronology associated with it, Ephrem draws attention to the inter-relatedness at a deep structural level of the Annunciation/conception, the Last Supper, and the Eucharist. Occasionally he makes the leap straight from Mary to the Eucharist, as:

> Mary has given us the Bread of Rest
> in place of that bread of toil which Eve provided.
>
> (*Unleavened Bread* 6:7)

Turning to the question of terminology, we need to focus our attention on a single verse in the annunciation narrative of Saint Luke's Gospel, Luke 1:35, where the angel Gabriel tells Mary 'The Holy Spirit shall come upon you, and the Power of the Most High shall overshadow you'.

Ephrem, in common with later West Syrian exegetical tradition, identifies the 'Power of the Most High' as the Word. In the Greek text this Power is to 'overshadow' (*episkiasei*) Mary; all the Syriac versions, however, employ the causative form of a verb connected etymologically with *gnona*, 'bridal chamber', the theme of the next chapter. This Syriac verb *aggen* is actually very difficult to translate; perhaps 'cover over' will suffice for our purposes. Ephrem already quotes Luke 1:35 with this verb in his Commentary on the Diatessaron, and it has an interesting background in Jewish Aramaic, for in one strand of the Palestinian Targum tradition it features in the Passover narrative of Exodus 12, translating the key Hebrew word *pasaḥ* (whence Pascha, Passover) in Exodus 12:23.[6] Another apparent link between Annunciation and Passover, it would seem—but it is not one that Ephrem takes up: although he knows some Targum traditions indirectly, this is one which he evidently did not know.

In the genuine works Ephrem is not particularly interested in this term *aggen*, even though it is already something of a technical term to the Syriac translators of the New Testament, and even though in later Syriac tradition, from the fifth century onwards, the term becomes a technical one to denote the activity of the Holy Spirit, among other places at the epiclesis during the Eucharistic Liturgy—yet a further link between Incarnation and Eucharist.

Ephrem, however, antedates these developments, but he does happen to arrive at exactly the same parallelism by quite a different way: instead of making use of the possibilities of the term *aggen*, he uses another word, also with a rich sacral background in Jewish Aramaic, namely the verb *shra*, 'take up residence, dwell'. It is this term that Ephrem regularly uses with reference to Christ's presence both in Mary's womb and in the consecrated Bread and Wine. Such usage is entirely apt when seen against the background of Jewish Aramaic where the verb is employed especially in connection with the Shekhina, the divine presence, and the *iqara*, divine glory.

It is time to look at some examples, first of all the passages where Christ is said to 'reside' (*shra*) in Mary's womb:[7]

> In Nisan the Lord of thunder
> in His mercy modified His might,
> descended and took up residence* in   *shra*
> Mary's womb
>
> *(Resurrection 4:10)*
>
> Blessed is He who took up residence in the womb
> and built there a temple wherein to dwell (John 2:21),
> a shrine in which to be,
> a garment in which He might shine out.
>
> *(Nativity 3:20)*

Since Ephrem, in common with many other early Syriac writers, often employs *shra* 'reside' in place of *aggen* when alluding to Luke 1:35 and John 1:14 (at both of which passages all the Syriac versions attest *aggen*), it is conceivable that the term *shra* is an archaism inherited by them from the very earliest period of Syriac Christianity, based on an oral, rather than a written, Gospel.[8] If there is anything in this suggestion, then we would have an exciting glimpse into the Aramaic prehistory of the written Greek, Gospel text.

For the use of this verb in a Eucharistic context we need only return once more to the tenth hymn on Faith:

> The Fire of compassion descended
> and took up residence★ in the Bread.   ★*shrat*
>
> *(Faith 10:12)*

and

> In Your Wine there resides★   ★*sharya*
> the Fire that is not drunk.
>
> *(Faith 10:8)*

As was to happen later with the term *aggen*, so too the term *shra* came to be extended to other salvific events: thus Ephrem uses it both of the action of Christ's body in the Jordan, and of the Holy Spirit upon the disciples at Pentecost *(Faith 74:12)*.

What then is the significance of this parallelism between Incarnation and Eucharist that Ephrem points to in a whole variety of different ways? Put schematically: just as the Divinity 'took up residence' in Mary's womb, so too does the divine 'hidden power' in the Bread and Wine 'take up residence' in the communicant. For this latter aspect we may turn to one of the Armenian Eucharistic hymns (47, lines 27–30):

> The Medicine of Life flew down from on high
> to reside in those worthy of it.
>
> Let us make holy our souls and thoughts
> in honour of His glory.

We hold God in our hands:
let there be no blemish in our bodies.
Once He has entered, He takes up residence with us,
so let us make ourselves holy within.

The comparison with Mary's womb in explicit in another hymn:

The Holy One took up residence in the womb in bod–
ily fashion,
Now He takes up residence in the mind, in spiritual
fashion.

(Nativity 4:130)

In another of the Nativity hymns we are intriguingly brought back
to the passover imagery, with a direct reference to Exodus 12:7:

At this feast of the Nativity
let each person wreathe the door of his heart
so that the Holy Spirit may delight in his door,
enter in and take up residence there;
then by the Spirit he will be made holy.

(Nativity 5:10)

And just as the residing of the Divinity in Mary's womb re-
sulted in her giving birth, so too the result of Communion, when
the 'hidden power' takes up residence anew in the communicant,
should also be birthgiving:

My mind, Lord, is barren of any birthgiving of new
things:
grant fruitfulness and birthgiving to my mind,
as You did to Hannah,
so that utterance, in the form of a child proceeding
from my mouth,
may be offered to You, just like Samuel, that barren
woman's son.

(Church 30:1)

As one of the Armenian hymns on the Eucharist puts it, the heart
of the communicant is nothing less than the actual bridal chamber

where Christ the Heavenly Bridegroom and the soul as bride meet:

> Wonderful is this bounty,
> that our Lord should reside in us continually:
> He has left the heavens and descended,
> let us make holy for Him the bridal chamber of our
>   hearts.

(*Armenian hymns* 47, lines 46–47)

It is to the theme of Christ the Bridegroom that we shall next turn.

7

THE BRIDAL CHAMBER OF THE HEART

IN THIS CHAPTER we shall be exploring a New Testament theme which proved to be both popular and influential in early Syriac Christianity: Christ the Bridegroom. That Ephrem should have a considerable amount to say on this topic will by now come as no surprise, but before turning to him it will be helpful to glance at the New Testament roots of the imagery. Three passages are of prime importance as far as Ephrem is concerned:

— Matthew 9:15 (with parallels in Mark 2:19 and Luke 5:34). This is Jesus' reply to the Pharisees' question to him about fasting: 'Can the children of the bridechamber fast ('mourn' in Matthew) while the bridegroom is with them?'

— John 3:29, where John the Baptist identifies himself, not as the Messiah, but rather as 'the friend of the Bridegroom to whom the bride belongs'.

— Matthew 25:1–13, the parable of the Wise and Foolish Virgins. Verse 10 is of particular significance here: 'while the foolish virgins were away buying oil, the bridegroom arrived; and those who were ready went in with him to the wedding feast'—or, as we shall shortly see, 'the bridal chamber'.

Other parables likening the Kingdom to a Wedding Feast may also be relevant, in particular Matthew 22, on the wedding garment (which we have already met at the end of Chapter Five).

In all three of the main passages mentioned the bridegroom is by implication to be identified as Christ. The bride is only mentioned in the second passage, and there the implicit identification is with Israel; the context of John's baptizing is also, as we shall see, of significance.

The first passage mentions the bridal chamber, *gnona*, while for the third the Syriac textual witnesses are divided. The only surviving Old Syriac manuscript here (Sinaiticus) has *beth meshtuta*, 'banquet', 'wedding feast', and the same sense is implied by the Peshitta's *beth ḥlula*. Many early Syriac writers, however, including Ephrem, know quite a different reading, *gnona*, 'bridal chamber', suggesting a much more intimate scenario.[1]

The term *gnona* is particularly important in Ephrem's religious vocabulary: it may refer to the Kingdom in its eschatololgical dimensions, or it may refer to the Kingdom as realized, or as realizable, here on earth by individuals. Where the reference is to the eschatological Kingdom (synonymous with Paradise in Ephrem's thought), then we are provided with another illustration of the relationship between events in historical time, here and now, and events in eschatological time: the betrothal is seen as taking place in historical time (whether the bride to be is collective or individual), while the marriage feast and the mystery of the consummation of the marriage in the bridal chamber belong to the eschaton.

In order to gain a better appreciation of Ephrem's very varied and imaginative use of this whole area of wedding imagery in the context of the spiritual life, it will be helpful once again to attempt a fairly schematized presentation, even though any schematization always runs the risk of fossilizing the dynamic fluidity of Ephrem's poetic thought. Our general movement will be from images of a collective betrothed bride—first Israel, then the Church—on to the individual bride, with the consequent interiorization of the imagery, and the heart itself as the bridal chamber.

ISRAEL AS THE BETROTHED

The Old Testament already provides abundant passages where Israel is depicted as betrothed to God, the betrothal having taken place at the time of the Covenant, the Lawgiving, on Mount Sinai. Ephrem describes the episode in the following terms:

Nisan the victorious month, which was sent by the
   Victorious One
was resplendent and victorious in Egypt,
delivering and escorting out the Royal Bride.
It sprinkled the ground before her with its abundance,
filling it with flowers scattered everywhere;
lightning served as torches that gave illumination
while thunder roared its acclaim;
the mountains skipped before her.
Blessed is the Exalted One who escorted the despised
   girl.

A chaste wedding feast took place in the Wilderness,
with the bridal chamber set on Mount Sinai.
The Holy One descended and took in betrothal
the daughter of Abraham His beloved friend.

(Resurrection 3:1–2)

For Ephrem and for any other Christian writer using this imagery there was a dilemma: since it is going to be the Church
which ultimately emerges as the Bride of Christ, there is the
problem of how precisely to relate these two Brides, Israel and
the Church. Among early Syriac writers we encounter two basically different conceptual models.[2]

What is clearly the earlier model (and more correct historically)
sees the Church as being constituted out of two elements, the
Jewish Nation or People, and the Gentile Nations or Peoples. Thus
Aphrahat writes: 'David married two kings' daughters, and Jesus
also married two kings' daughters—the assembly of the People
and the assembly of the Peoples' (*Demonstration 21:13*).

The second conceptual model sees the Church as being gathered solely from the Peoples, or Gentiles. According to this model
'the Church of the Peoples' has simply taken the place of Israel as
the Bride of God. It is the second conceptual model that became
predominant in Syriac tradition, and Ephrem already reflects it
later on in the third hymn on the Resurrection (and indeed usually elsewhere too). It is probable that the parable of the vineyard

(Matthew 21:33–41) played a role in the shift from the one model to the other.[3]

How does this change of intended Brides take place? Ephrem unfolds this in the rest of the hymn whose opening has already been quoted: there are two stages by which the original Bride (Israel) rejects the Bridegroom (God). First, the betrothed Bride commits adultery on the very threshold of the bridal chamber; Ephrem refers of course to the episode of the Golden Calf at the very foot of Mount Sinai (Exodus 32). Then secondly, the betrothed Bride, having been forgiven and re-instated, is given a second chance, when the royal Bridegroom's Son (that is, Christ) comes to see His betrothed. Here, then, is how Ephrem continues the hymn:

> Great was the horror when all of a sudden
> the Bride played the adulteress in her very bridal chamber.
> Moses the betrother had gone up to the Bridegroom
> and a stranger had entered the bridal chamber:
> the Bride rejected the King and fell in love with the Calf.
> Blessed is the Pure One who put in writing her dismissal.
>
> *(Resurrection 3:2)*

As a consequence of her adulterous act God does not bring Israel at once into the promised land, lest she prove a bad example to the Nations (Gentiles) living there. The next generation, however, He reinstates:

> He brought up her daughter in her place,
> giving her the adornments that had belonged to her mother.
> He warned her of her mother's impurity
> and promised her that if she was chaste
> the King's Son would be betrothed to her.
>
> *(Resurrection 3:3)*

In the fourth stanza the King's Son arrives to meet His betrothed: the scene is the entry into Jerusalem:

> Joyful Nisan was sent to the daughter as to the mother
> in order to crown this daughter of Sarah.
> And there went out to meet the King's Son
> a great procession, in front of the Bridegroom,
> so that the Bride might rejoice in her Betrothed.
> The lame leaped like rams,
> the blind were illumined like lamps,
> there was acclamation along with the palm branches.[4]
> Blessed is He who made chaste the infatuated one.
>
> The daughter of Sarah beheld the King's Son,
> she saw He was chaste, and she became downcast;
> she saw He was pure, and so she played sick,
> for she was used to adulterers;
> she accused Him so that she might not herself be ac-
> cused . . .

> (*Resurrection 3:4–5*)

Having been rejected by His betrothed, the Bridegroom has to turn elsewhere (stanza 7):

> When the King's Son perceived her wicked behaviour
> He came and took in betrothal the Church of the Na-
> tions,
> for He had tested her love and her loyalty;
> He mingled her with Himself, and was mingled with
> her.

The rejection by the betrothed Bride (Israel) of her intended Bridegroom is again depicted as taking place at Christ's entry into Jerusalem in another hymn where Ephrem's choice of phraseology deliberately links the event with the parable of the wise and foolish virgins:

> The Passover feast and Nisan, the two brothers,
> were joyful messengers of good tidings;
> they ran and proclaimed to the daughter,

just as they had done earlier to her mother:
'Behold, the Bridegroom is at the door,
come out to meet Him'.
She beheld Him, and He did not please her:
she was irritated because He was holy,
she trembled because He was the Saviour,
she was astonished because He was so lowly.

(*Crucifixion 1:2*)

This scenario is still preserved in the liturgical texts for Palm Sunday, the Sunday of Hosanna, and features in particular in two delightful anonymous poems where the Church and the Synagogue (or Sion) dispute,[5] in alternating stanzas, their respective rights to be Bride to the heavenly Bridegroom in the following vein:

Synagogue: Moses who wrote out my dowry is witness
that the finger of the Most High sealed my
marriage document.
The Father has entrusted me with His
house,
for I am the heiress.

Church: Moses whom you invoke is indeed witness
—that he saw your adultery and so broke
the tablets.
Adulteresses do not inherit:
your document is annulled, so why do you
boast?

But the entry into Jerusalem is not the only setting within the Gospel narrative where Ephrem introduces Christ as the Bridegroom: the theme is also employed in connection with John the Baptist. This might at first sight seem surprising, but as usual Ephrem is simply building on hints already provided in the New Testament text, in this case John 3:29, where John the Baptist refers to himself as 'the friend of the Bridegroom to whom the bride belongs'.

In one of the hymns on Virginity Ephrem weaves together three different Gospel themes: the Baptist as friend of the True

Bridegroom (John 3:29), and as 'lamp' (John 5:35), and the 'lamps' of the Parable of the virgins (Matthew 25):

> The feeble lamp is a symbol of John:
> both exist only for a limited time;
> the lamp is not the bridegroom of the eye,
> nor is John the bridegroom of the Church.
> They are friends of the two bridegrooms (the sun and
>   Christ)
> and beloved by the two brides;
> they were not bridegrooms, but icons
> of the Unique Bridegroom.
> The eye sees with the help of a lamp
> which resembles the sun, its true bridegroom;
> the Church beheld in John
> the semblance of her true Partner.
> Oil (*meshha*) enriches the light
> of lamps, as though in symbol;
> Christ (*meshiha*) enriches the lamps of the virgins who
>   are betrothed to Him.
>
> (*Virginity 5:9*)

Already implicit in this passage, but more recognizable in the next, is the idea of John the Baptist as unveiling the Bridegroom to the expectant bride:

> John the betrother became aware
> that the bride of his Lord was looking to him
> as if he—a mere servant—was himself that Lord,
> so he revealed that he was but the servant;
> he showed his mortal nature,
> he showed his humble role,
> he showed her both the glory and his own lowly estate,
> when he told her that he was not even worthy
> to loosen the strap of the Bridegroom's sandal.
> Blessed is He who instructed John thus to teach her.
>
> (*Heresies 24:6*)

The theme of the Baptism of Christ as the unveiling of the heavenly Bridegroom was to be taken up by later poets and it is to be found in a developed form in the liturgical texts both for Epiphany and for the Consecration of the Church which features in the liturgical calendar just before the period of the Annunciation (Western Advent);[6] a fine early example can be found in a popular anonymous dialogue poem (between John the Baptist and Jesus) whose opening reads:[7]

> My imagination wafted me to the Jordan
> where I beheld a wonder
> when the glorious Bridegroom was revealed
> to make a marriage feast for the Bride and to sanctify
> her.

In passing it might be noticed that neither in this poem, nor anywhere in Ephrem's genuine writings do we find the theme of the replacement of the one bride by the other, the Synagogue by the Church, associated with Christ's baptism (as opposed to the Entry into Jerusalem); this would appear to be a later development: it is prominent, for example, in Jacob of Serugh's homilies on the Baptism.[8] As far as Christ's baptism is concerned Ephrem's interest is solely in the betrothal of the Church; and in his eyes it was all the more appropriate that this event should have taken place there, given the presence of water at the various betrothals in the Old Testament which took place beside wells (*Commentary on the Diatessaron 3:17*).

THE CHURCH AS BRIDE

The movement from the image of Christ as the Bridegroom who is revealed at his baptism in the Jordan to that of the Church as the Bride at Christian baptism is found in the fifth of Ephrem's hymns on the Fast. He envisages baptisms as taking place after the Lenten Fast, at Easter, and this gives him the opportunity to allude also to the Entry into Jerusalem, whose importance in the context of bridal imagery we have already seen; he also alludes, once again, to the parable of the virgins:

> Assiduous fasts have stirred themselves
> to become companions to guide the Bride of the King

so that she might be escorted and come
to the wedding feast all in white,
that she might be baptized there, and so shine out:
her crowns will come from her companions,
her adornment will come from her fasts.
She shall proceed amidst shouts of hosanna,
before her shall shine a lamp with enduring oil.
Blessed is He who sent and escorted the Bride
of His First-Born Son, so that she might come
to the Bridal Chamber of His Light.

(Fast 5:1)

Thus one of the many aspects of Christian baptism is betrothal to Christ. In the case of consecrated virgins this was understood very literally, and it is likely that vows of virginity were normally made at baptism (which in Ephrem's time probably took place more often than not in adulthood). Ephrem frequently speaks of virgins as being 'betrothed to Christ' (*Virginity 5:10*), 'betrothed to the Living One' (*Virginity 24:5*), as having exchanged 'a temporal bridal chamber for The Bridal Chamber whose blessed joy never departs' (*Virginity 24:5*)

As usual in his hymns, Ephrem moves very freely from the collective to the individual, from the Church to the individual Christian, and then back from the individual to the collective. This appears very clearly in the way Ephrem handles a further New Testament passage into which he introduces the theme of Christ the Bridegroom, the wedding feast at Cana (John 2):

Blessed are you, Cana,
for it was the Bridegroom from on high
whom your bridegroom invited, whose wine ran out;
he invited the Guest who himself invited the Nations
to a wedding feast of joy and life in Eden.

(Virginity 16:2)

Or Cana herself may speak:

Together with my guests will I give thanks
because Christ has held me worthy to invite Him

—the Heavenly Bridegroom who has come down and
   invited all,
and I too have been invited to enter His pure wedding
   feast.
Among men on earth shall I acknowledge Him as
   Bridegroom,
for there is none other beside;
His Bridal Chamber is established for eternity,
and His Wedding Feast is provided with riches
and is needful of nothing,
not like my own feast, whose shortcomings He has
   fulfilled.

(Virginity 33:4)

In another poem on this subject Ephrem adds an important
new element: Christ's own Wedding Feast is the Eucharist, where
the bride is both the Church and the individual soul. This hymn,
however, does not just interweave features from the two wedding
feasts, that of Cana and the Eucharist, for in the opening stanza
Ephrem introduces yet a third wedding feast, one of praise, which
he invites Christ to grace with His presence. This third wedding
feast is itself the outcome of the Eucharistic wedding feast:

I have invited You, Lord, to a wedding feast of song,
but the wine—the utterance of praise—at our feast has
   failed.
You are the guest who filled the jars with good wine,
fill my mouth with Your praise.

The wine that was in the jars was akin and related to
this eloquent Wine that gives birth to praise,
seeing that wine too gave birth to praise
from those who drank it and beheld the wonder.

You who are so just, if at a wedding feast not Your own
You filled six jars with good wine,
do You at this wedding feast fill, not the jars,
but the ten thousand ears with its sweetness.

Jesus, You were invited to a wedding feast of others,
here is Your own pure and fair wedding feast: gladden
   Your rejuvenated people,
for Your guests too, O Lord, need
Your songs: let Your harp utter.

The soul is Your bride, the body Your bridal chamber,
Your guests are the senses and the thoughts.
And if a single body is a wedding feast for You,
how great is Your banquet for the whole Church!

(Faith 14:1–5)

Ephrem then continues in the next two stanzas with mention of Mount Sinai where Moses betrothed Israel to God, but where 'the bride played false in her own bridal chamber'.

Since Ephrem's Christian community naturally did not consist entirely of consecrated 'virgins' (the term in Syriac covers men as well as women), he often identifies the bride simply as the soul: Christ 'has come to be betrothed to souls' (*Virginity 25:16*), and in the hymn just quoted 'the soul is Your bride, the body Your bridal chamber'. In this whole stanza we should note both the very honoured role that Ephrem accords to the body, and, at the same time, the way he maintains the tension between individual and collective. In that stanza's first line the bride of Christ is each individual soul at the wedding feast of the Eucharist: Christ the Bridegroom here enters the body of the communicant, and so the body can in a very literal sense be described as the very bridal chamber. The reference to Israel's adultery at Sinai, which follows immediately in the next stanza, is primarily intended as a warning to the Eucharistic bride—the soul—not to behave in the same sort of way in her own bridal chamber, the body.

Then in the second half of the stanza Ephrem moves from the individual bride, the soul, to the collective bride, the Church; and with the movement from individual to collective we should probably also understand a movement from historical time to eschatological time: each individual soul is the bride at each celebration of the Eucharistic Liturgy that takes place in historical time, while the collective Church is the bride at the eschatological wedding feast.

In the light of this we could perhaps formulate the relationship of the collective to the individual in Ephrem's thought somewhat along the following lines. A collective sense will predominate wherever the event Ephrem is describing has paradigmatic character: episodes where he is interested primarily in the inner significance of what is happening, and where the outward narrative of events serves just as a vehicle for conveying that inner significance; in itself it need not have any definite link with actual historical events in historical time. The outward narrative is story, rather than history, but that story tells about an inward truth, an inner reality. In other words, where Ephrem's focus is primarily on the collective, whether it be Adam, the bride, or whoever, he will be concerned pre-eminently with sacred time, even though the outward narrative (as in the Sinai episode) may sometimes belong to historical time.

When, however, Ephrem's interest shifts from the paradigmatic to what is seen as dependent on that paradigm, he will move from the collective to the individual, and from sacred time to historical time. We have already had occasion to observe Ephrem's love of underlying symmetrical patterns, the complementarity and balance between the First Adam and the Second Adam, between the descent of the Divinity and the ascent of humanity. So too in the present context we have a dynamic pattern of movement from the collective in sacred primordial time to the individual in historical time, and then back to the collective in sacred eschatological time, where the potential implied in primordial time is actually fulfilled. But because both potential and fulfilment belong to sacred time, they can also be seen by the individual 'luminous eye' of faith as already present at any point in linear time.

MARY AS BRIDE

In Ephrem's thought the Virgin Mary is seen very much as a model for the ideal pattern of relationship between the human individual and God: she fulfils the potential that Eve failed to achieve. Thus it is no surprise to find that she too is Christ's bride:

> She alone is Your mother,
> but she is Your sister, with everyone else.
> She was Your mother, she was Your sister,
> she was Your bride too,
> along with all chaste souls.
> You, who are Your mother's beauty
> Yourself adorned her with everything.

(Nativity 11:2)

But Mary is the only bride for whom the sacred marriage is literally consummated in the 'bridal chamber' of her body in historical time:

> She was, by her virgin nature, Your bride already
> before You came; she conceived in a manner
> quite beyond nature, after You had come,
> O Holy One; and she was a virgin
> when she gave birth to You in most holy fashion.

(Nativity 11:3)

In one other nativity hymn Ephrem speaks of Mary as bride, and once again we have an allusion to the wedding feast at Cana:

> Cry out for joy, you bridegrooms and your brides!
> Blessed is the Child whose mother became
> a bride to the Holy One.
> Happy the wedding feast
> where you, Christ, are in its midst:
> for even though its wine
> should run out all of a sudden,
> thanks to You it will be abundant again.

(Nativity 8:18)

THE BRIDAL CHAMBER OF THE HEART

So far we have been concerned with the body as the bridal chamber where the soul meets the Bridegroom. The imagery may also be interiorized, in which case the bridal chamber is no longer located in the body, but in the heart, the very centre of the human person. When Ephrem speaks of the 'heart' he is of course following the biblical concept of the human person, according to which the heart denotes the seat, not just of the emotions, but also of the intellectual faculties as well. Under the influence of Greek philosophical concepts European Christian tradition has tended to see the mind as quite separate from the heart, and so we need consciously to recall this more integrated biblical view of the human personality that is Ephrem's.

Ephrem uses the phrase 'bridal chamber of the heart' on two occasions. One of these is in a Eucharistic context, in a hymn already quoted at the end of chapter 6:

> How wonderful is this abundance
> that the Lord should reside in us continually,
> for He has left the heavens and descended:
> let us make holy for Him the bridal chamber of our
>   hearts.
>
> (*Armenian hymns* 47, lines 46–7)

In the other passage Ephrem is contrasting outward and inward circumcision, of the body and of the heart:

> With a circumcised heart
> uncircumcision becomes holy:
> in the bridal chamber of such a person's heart
> the Creator resides.
>
> (*Virginity* 44:20)

In the light of Ephrem's usage of bridal imagery elsewhere we can legitimately see two important resonances here. On the one hand, outward circumcision will refer to Judaism, the bride who committed adultery in her own bridal chamber on Mt Sinai. On the other hand, it is a standard understanding of early Syriac Christianity that circumcision is replaced by baptism as the rite of entry into the community—and baptism too, as we have seen, is another betrothal. Taking these two resonances together, one can see that what Ephrem is conveying here in very compact form is schematically the following: the Divinity that resided on Mt Sinai,

but which was rejected by the intended bride, Israel, now resides
in the heart of the baptized.

Once bridal imagery has been internalized an obvious further
step for Ephrem is to associate it with his much loved image of
the mirror:

> In the mirror of the commandments
> I will behold my interior face
> so that I may wash off the dirt on my soul
> and clean away the filth of my mind,
> lest the Holy One to whom I am betrothed sees me
> and stands back from me in abhorrence.
>
> (*Armenian hymns 6*, lines 42–47)

In another poem Ephrem internalizes bridal imagery in quite a
different way: this is to be found in an important hymn on Prayer
and Faith (*Hymns on Faith 20*). The first two verses, significantly
replete with references to conception and birthgiving, give the
setting:

> To You, Lord, do I offer my faith with my voice,
> for prayer and entreaty can both
> be conceived in the mind
> and brought to birth in silence, without using the voice.
> If the womb holds back the child, then both mother
>   and child will die;
> may my mouth, Lord, not hold back my faith
> with the result that the one perish and the other is
>   quenched,
> the two of them perishing, each because of the other.

After further illustrating this birth-giving process from examples taken from nature, Ephrem turns to the balance that is required between the internal practice of prayer and the external
manifestation and proclamation of faith. Both prayer and faith
are betrothed brides, but they have different roles: one lives in-
doors, the other out of doors. In the first of the next pair of
stanzas to be quoted Ephrem alludes to Matthew 6:6, where Jesus
speaks of the need to pray in the inner chamber with the door

closed. In Ephrem the inner chamber has become that of the heart:[9]

> Prayer that has been refined is a virgin in 'the inner
>   chamber':
> if she pass the 'door' of the mouth, she is like one gone
>   astray.
> Truth is her bridal chamber, love her crown,
> stillness and silence are the trusty eunuchs at her door.
>
> She is betrothed to the King's Son; let her not wantonly
>   come out,
> but let Faith, who is publicly the bride, be escorted
> in the streets, carried on the back of the voice
> from the mouth to another bridal chamber, that of
>   the ear.

(Faith 20:6–7)

The necessity for Faith to come out into public is made clear in the next stanza:

> For it is written that there were many who believed in
>   our Lord,
> but out of fear their voices dishonoured faith:
> although their hearts confessed,
> yet our Lord considered those who kept silent along
>   with those who denied.

(Faith 20:8)

The following stanzas of this twentieth hymn on Faith provide a connection with one of the important themes of the next chapter. Ephrem moves from one inseparable pair, Prayer and Faith, to another, Love and Truth, who (as we have already seen) 'are wings that cannot be separated'. For the heart, Truth and Love should be like a person's eyes or legs, working together in harmony. Just as the feet do not walk in two different directions, nor should the heart be divided, walking along both the paths of light and of darkness: rather, the heart must be 'single', *iḥidaya*, in readiness for the 'single Bridegroom', *ḥathna iḥidaya*.

8

THE ASCETIC IDEAL:
SAINT EPHREM AND
PROTO-MONASTICISM

SYRIAN 'PROTO-MONASTICISM':
A FORGOTTEN TRADITION

THE SIXTH-CENTURY SYRIAC LIFE of Saint Ephrem, and later tradition in general, portrays the saint as a monk. This is already hinted at in Palladius' Lausiac History (written about 419/20), and specifically stated by the fifth-century Church historian Sozomen who says (III.16) that Ephrem 'devoted his life to the monastic philosophy'.

These later writers and their readers will have associated Ephrem with the monasticism that sprung up in Egypt and spread northwards to Syria and elsewhere with astonishing rapidity in the course of the fourth and fifth centuries. It is in order to associate Ephrem in a tangible way with prestigious Egyptian monasticism that the sixth-century Life has Ephrem actually travel to Egypt to visit Saint Bishoi.

This later picture is misleading, for two reasons. First, in that it is anachronistic, and secondly (and fundamentally more important) because it ignores and neglects the existence of a native Syrian tradition of the consecrated life which may be termed 'proto-monasticism'. It was a tradition which later, for the most part, became fused with the Egyptian monastic tradition.

Owing to the immense prestige which Egyptian monasticism soon acquired, subsequent Syrian tradition actually forgot its own native roots, and attributed the origins of Syrian and Mesopotamian monasticism entirely to Egyptian sources. How later Syrian monastic tradition thus sold its own birthright to Egypt can be seen from two remarkable examples. First is the case of the 'Macarian Homilies', an influential corpus of homilies and treatises on the spiritual life whose Syrian and Mesopotamian provenance has had to be re-discovered by modern scholarship, for the manuscript tradition, from an early date, had more or less consistently attributed them to one or the other of the Egyptian Macarii.

The second example concerns the standard later Syriac tradition concerning the origins of monasticism in Syria and Mesopotamia. According to this tradition monasticism was brought to Mesopotamia by the Egyptian monk Mar Awgen (Eugenios), with his seventy disciples. In the cycle of Lives of Mar Awgen and his disciples we have detailed accounts of how Egyptian-style monasticism was implanted in Mesopotamia in the fourth century. On closer examination, however, these traditions turn out to be unattested before the early Arab period, and the Lives themselves lack any really reliable historical data (although they are rich in local geographical information).

Thus one of the reasons why later texts speak of Ephrem as a monk is because later generations had simply forgotten about the existence of the native Syrian/Mesopotamian proto-monasticism. Another reason lies in the fact that a number of texts which are clearly familiar with Egyptian monasticism came to be associated with the name of Ephrem himself. Modern scholars are in fact divided on the question of which, if any, of these 'monastic' texts belong to Ephrem: Arthur Vööbus in particular would extend the net of works he considers genuine far wider than does Dom Edmund Beck, but, for reasons which cannot be elaborated upon here, it would seem that the latter scholar is a far more satisfactory guide on this particular matter.

Taking as a basis only those works of Ephrem concerning whose authenticity there is no good reason to doubt, it appears that Ephrem only came into contact with the exported Egyptian monastic tradition towards the end of his life, and perhaps only during his last ten years, in Edessa. He himself was no more a monk (in the formal sense) than was his older contemporary Aphrahat abbot of the famous monastery of Mar Mattai in north Iraq (to cite but another figment of the medieval imagination).

But if Ephrem does not have anything directly to do with Egyptian monasticism, he does very much belong to this native Syrian ascetic tradition which I am calling 'proto-monasticism'. It is to certain prominent aspects of this tradition that we shall now turn.

In order to discover something of the character and riches of this tradition it will be necessary to extend our vision beyond the genuine corpus of Ephrem's writings to some earlier Syriac writers, in particular Aphrahat, whose sixth Demonstration is of particular importance.[1]

This sixth Demonstration happens immediately to highlight a terminological difficulty which we shall have to face. The English translation of this work gives it the title 'On Monks', and the Latin too renders it *de monachis*. Such a rendering is, however, anachronistic and highly misleading. The Syriac original in fact has 'On the *bnay qyama*', literally 'On the children of the *qyama*', that is to say 'members of the *qyama*', or Covenant', as it is usually translated (though, as we shall see, this rendering is disputed by some).

It will, accordingly, be helpful to survey briefly the various main terms in Syriac which are employed with reference to some form or other of the consecrated life, the technical terms of this proto-monastic tradition.[2] Four terms are of central importance. (1) *Iḥidaya*. This is the most important, as well as most complex, of all. I leave it untranslated at present, but we shall return to it later to examine it in detail. (2) *Bthulta, bthula*, 'virgin', both feminine and masculine, and the abstract *bthuluta* 'virginity'. Ephrem frequently uses the masculine form to denote figures such as the prophet Elijah and John the Baptist. (3) *Qaddisha*, literally 'holy', and the abstract *qaddishuta*. In early Syriac writers, however, these terms have a much more specialized sense: a *qaddisha* is a married person who abstains from sexual intercourse. Such a meaning for *qaddisha* might at first sight seem surprising, but if one turns to the narrative of the Lawgiving on Mount Sinai, the origin of this usage becomes apparent: in Exodus 19:10 God tells Moses 'Go to the people and sanctify (*qaddshu*) them', but in verse 15 we find Moses telling the people 'do not approach your wives'. *Qaddishuta*, in the technical sense of abstinence from marital intercourse, can be a temporary or a permanent state. Ephrem knows the Jewish tradition that in the Ark, during the period of the Flood, Noah and his family, along with all the animals, preserved *qaddishuta*:

> And God said to Noah, 'Go out, you and your wife, your sons and your sons' wives' (Gen. 8:16). Those whom God had caused to come in singly, to preserve *qaddishuta* in the Ark, He caused to leave in couples, in order to multiply and be fruitful in creation. He also said concerning the animals which had preserved *qaddishuta* in the Ark, 'Take out with you every animal that was with you . . . . and let them give birth on the earth and be fruitful and multiply on it' (Gen. 8:17–18).
>
> (*Commentary on Genesis 6:12*)

The *qaddishe* of Ephrem's own day are likely to have been people who had taken permanent vows of abstinence, possibly made at (adult) baptism.

(4) This is the term we have already met, *qyama*, often found in conjunction with *bar, bath, bnay, bnath,* 'son(s), daughter(s)', that is, members of the *qyama*. The term is conventionally translated by 'Covenant', and as justification for this one can point to the Peshitta Old Testament, where *qyama* regularly translates Hebrew *brith*, 'covenant'.

Whether or not this understanding is correct (and it may well be), we can safely dismiss one theory that has been put forward by some scholars who opt for *qyama* meaning 'covenant'; according to this view the *bnay qyama* of the early Syriac Church had direct roots in the Qumran community, which termed itself both a *brith* and a *yahad* (etymologically connected with our first term, *ihidaya*). No firm evidence, however, for any such link with the Qumran community exists, and the hypothesis for such a connection is best left on one side.

Besides 'covenant' there are in fact several other possible explanations of the meaning *qyama* in this context.

—It has been suggested that in this context it has the sense of 'resurrection', and so the *bnay qyama* would be those who anticipate the resurrection. Although anticipation of the resurrection life is certainly an important motivating force behind early Syriac ascetic ideals, this particular explanation of *qyama* is problematic, since the word for 'resurrection' from this root in Syriac is the feminine form *qyamta,* not *qyama.*

—Another suggestion is that *qyama* means 'stance', in particular the 'stance' of angels, who do not sleep. Again, although the angelic life is another important ingredient of Syrian protomonasticism, there seems to be insufficient support for this meaning of *qyama.*

—A fourth possibility again points to the idea of 'standing' as underlying *qyama,* but in this case the word is seen as corresponding in particular to Hebrew *ma'amad* and Latin *statio,* both technical terms, the former denoting a group of people who undertake to perform certain liturgical duties, and the latter meaning 'vigil', 'watch' (thence developing into 'fast').

This is not the place to go any further into the problem, and here it will suffice to mention that there is evidence that the *qyama* was sometimes understood as a vow, either of *bthuluta* 'virginity', or of *qaddishuta* 'sexual abstinence in marriage'—a vow which was probably made at the same time as baptism when this took place in adulthood.

In any case the *bnay qyama* would appear to be a group of people who led some form of consecrated life, and whose common denominator was probably the fact that they had all undertaken a vow of chastity, whether as 'virgins', or as *qaddishe* in the technical sense of this word. This group, which could also be referred to simply as the *qyama,*[3] seem to have formed the core of the local church community; no doubt the priests and bishop will have been drawn from among their number, but in the early period (which includes Ephrem's lifetime) the clergy and the *qyama* will by no means have been coterminous.

From Aphrahat we learn that the members of the *qyama* lived in small associations, sometimes of men and women together (though this was frowned upon by Aphrahat), forming house communities or informal religious communes. They were essentially a feature of town and village life, a far remove from the Egyptian monastic model of *anachoresis* or withdrawal from town and village to the desert, whether singly, on the Antonian model, or in communities, following Pachomius.

It is time to return to the first term, *ihidaya*, which was left untranslated. In later monastic terminology *ihidaya* means a 'solitary', someone who leads an eremitical, or semi-eremitical, life (attached nonetheless to a community, though not living in it). It stands in contrast to the term *dayraya*, a monk living in a monastery. Since, however, *ihidaya* was often used to translate Greek *monachos*, in later texts *ihidaya* can sometimes serve as a synonym with *dayraya*. But as far as Aphrahat and Ephrem are concerned, *ihidaya* has nothing directly to do with *monachos* in the sense of 'monk', and neither writer yet knows the term *dayraya*.

What then is the meaning of *ihidaya* in the context of early Syrian proto-monasticism?

There would appear to be three basic ideas behind the term *ihidaya*: singular, individual, unique; single-minded, not divided in heart; and single in the sense of unmarried, celibate.

In the Syriac New Testament *Ihidaya* is above all a title of Christ, translating Greek *Monogenes*, Only-Begotten; but the term is found in other contexts as well in both the Syriac and Aramaic Bible. Thus in the Wisdom of Solomon 10:1 the term refers to Adam: 'It was Wisdom which preserved the ancestral father, the *ihidaya*, who had been created in the world'. In this sense it is a term which has an important background in the Jewish Aramaic Targumim where, not only are the Patriarchs sometimes described as *ihidaye*, but so too is Adam in the Palestinian Targum at Genesis 3:22. Here the Hebrew (along with Septuagint and Peshitta) has 'Behold, Adam has become like one of us, knowing good and evil', but the Palestinian Targum provides something very different: 'Behold the first Adam whom I created is single (*ihiday*) in the world, just as I am single (*Ihiday*) in the heights of heaven'. Thus already in Judaism we have the term *ihidaya* used both of God and of man, and it can be seen as eminently appropriate that in Christian texts the Second Adam should be *Ihidaya*, just as was the

First Adam.

To be 'single' is also to be single-minded, in other words, not to be divided, in the way that Adam's will was 'divided' when he stole and ate the forbidden fruit (*Crucifixion 8:2*); it is also 'a divided heart' that goes in for 'investigating' the hidden Divinity (*Faith 66:7*).

The third meaning, of 'celibate', also has a background in Jewish Aramaic. In Syriac we may simply cite Aphrahat, Demonstration 6:4: 'My beloved *iḥidaye* who do not marry . . .' It is evident from various passages in Aphrahat that these *iḥidaye* have also undertaken a vow of chastity, although exactly how they are to be related to the *bnay qyama* and the *bthule* is not clear.

Celibacy and single-mindedness were seen as closely linked by many circles in the early Church, sometimes taking Paul's words in I Corinthians 7:34, about the married person being 'divided up', as a starting point:[4] the unmarried person is undivided, and so can concentrate on God. Aphrahat expresses this idea in a famous passage in *Demonstration 18:10*, where he is commenting on Genesis 2:24, 'a man shall leave his father and mother':[5]

> Who is it who leaves father and mother to take a wife?
> The meaning is as follows: as long as a man has not
> taken a wife, he loves and reveres God his Father and
> the Holy Spirit his Mother, and he has no other love.
> But when a man takes a wife, then he leaves his Father
> and his Mother.

Two further connotations of the term *iḥidaya* are worth noting. When seeking for models in the Bible and in Judaism for the consecrated life that lies at the roots of monasticism, people in the fourth century pointed to two places in particular: Psalm 68:6, and Philo's description of the Jewish community known as the Therapeutai. Eusebius' commentary on the Psalms, dating from between 330 and 340, happens to contain the earliest literary reference to the Greek word *monachos* in the sense of 'monk'. The Hebrew text of the psalm in question has 'God causes the *yaḥid*, the single person, to dwell in a house', and Eusebius, commenting on the various Greek translations of *yaḥid*, 'single', says that

the passage refers to those who progress in Christ, namely the
monachoi, monks.[6] Syriac readers would also have found it easy to
link this passage with the consecrated life of the *iḥidaye*, since the
Peshitta has already rendered the Hebrew word there by *iḥidaya*
(the translator will have understood it in the sense of 'celibate,
bachelor').

In Eusebius' earlier work, the *Ecclesiastical History*, he has a passage on the Jewish Therapeutai, whom the Fathers regularly saw as
an antecedent for monasticism. Eusebius in this passage only uses
the term *monasterion*, not yet *monachos*, but the early Syriac translation, which may well already have been known to Ephrem, makes
considerable use of the term *iḥidaye* in rendering this passage on
the Therapeutai.[7]

The imitation of Christ was seen by Ephrem as the aim of all
Christians, but for the consecrated life of the *iḥidaya*, Christ the
Iḥidaya par excellence serves in a very special way as the model.
John the Baptist is already 'an *iḥidaya*, the proclaimer of the *Iḥidaya*'
(Commentary on the Diatessaron 1:16). At baptism those who are
embarking on a consecrated life 'put on Christ the *Iḥidaya* and so
become *iḥidaye*:

> See, people being baptized,
> becoming virgins and *qaddishe*,
> having gone down to the font,
> been baptized and put on
> that single *Iḥidaya*
>
> (*Epiphany 8:16*)

And rather earlier, Aphrahat had spoken of 'The *Iḥidaya* from the
bosom of the Father who gives joy to all the *iḥidaye*' (Demonstration 6:6). The passage continues as follows, introducing the
bridal imagery so much loved by Ephrem as well: 'There there
will be neither male nor female, servant or free (Galatians 3:28),
but all are children of the Most High, all are pure virgins betrothed
to Christ, their lamps shining out there as they enter the bridal
chamber together with the Bridegroom'.

We can begin to see that this key term of the Syrian proto-
monastic tradition is extremely rich in its various connotations.

The *iḥidaya* is a follower and imitator of Christ the *Iḥidaya* par excellence; he is single-minded for Christ; his heart is single and not divided; he is single as Adam was single when he was created; he is single in the sense of celibate.

MOTIVATION

If we are properly to appreciate the ascetic ideal that underlies a great deal of early Syriac Christianity, we need to look at the motivating forces that lie behind this native Syrian proto-monastic tradition, with its emphasis on virginity and sexual abstinence.

Some modern writers have supposed that this ideal implied a thoroughly dualist view of the world, one which regarded anything to do with the flesh as evil. Others have preferred to see the specific influence of Manichaeism at work here. But while it is possible that in some circles such influences were indeed present, it is manifest that this does not apply to the Christian community to which Ephrem himself belonged (and probably as an *iḥidaya*, though of this we cannot be certain). On many occasions Ephrem specifically disassociates himself, and the Christian community to which he belongs, from Marcionite and Manichaean views of marriage as something 'foul'.[8]

What lie behind the ascetic ideal of Syrian proto-monasticism are in fact three much more positive conceptual models:
—the model of Christ as the Bridegroom to whom individual Christians are betrothed at baptism;
—the model of baptism as a return to Paradise (in the Genesis narrative Adam and Eve did not cohabit until after the Fall and their expulsion from Paradise);
—the model of the baptismal life as the marriageless life of angels (Luke 20:35–6).

Since we have already considered the first model at some length, nothing more need be added here, though it is worth drawing attention to a passage in the Gospel of Thomas, a work which is generally agreed by scholars to have an origin in second-century Syria, and perhaps in a Semitic language (though it now survives only in Coptic and in some Greek fragments). In Logion 75 we encounter the words 'Many are standing at the door, but the 'solitary ones' are the ones who will enter the bridal chamber'. For the word 'solitary ones' the Coptic employs the Greek loan-word *monachos*, but this is certainly not meant in the later sense of 'monks'; rather, it corresponds exactly to Syriac *iḥidaya*.

As far as the second conceptual model is concerned, we have likewise already seen how central to Ephrem's way of thinking is the idea of baptism as re-entry into Paradise. The theme is indeed a recurrent one in all early Syriac texts, and is by no means confined to Saint Ephrem.

The ideal of the angelic life was just as popular in Syrian proto-monasticism as it was later to become in monastic circles. This too probably has its roots in Jewish ascetic groups around the turn of the Christian era. In the influential book of Daniel the angelic beings are described as *'ire*, 'Wakers' or 'Watchers', and as *qaddishin*, 'holy ones'. To a Syriac reader the term 'Waker' would readily be associated with the parable of the virgins in Matthew 25, with its emphasis on the need for wakefulness (25:13). But this association is not the main one to give emphasis to the marriageless character of the angelic life; for this, Luke 20:35–36 is of key importance, and it is of significance that the Old Syriac translation gives even more prominence to the marriageless life of angels as something to be anticipated on earth than does the Greek original. The Old Syriac reads here: 'Those who have become worthy to receive that world (i.e. the Kingdom) and that resurrection from the deads do not marry, nor can they die, for they have been made equal with the angels'.

But it is not only the angels, and their imitators on earth, who are 'Wakers', for Christ himself is 'the Wakeful One who has come to make us wakers on earth' (*Nativity 21:4*). Ephrem makes a great deal of the contrast between spiritual wakefulness and the sleep of sin:

> The Wakers rejoice today
>> for the Wakeful One has come to wake us up:
> on this night who shall sleep
>> when all creation is awake?

Because Adam introduced into the world
   the sleep of death in sins,
the Wakeful One came down to wake us up
   from being submerged in sin.

(Nativity 1:61–62)

At baptism the baptized 'put on the Wakeful One in the waters' (*Epiphany 4:8*), and so themselves become, in potential at any rate, 'wakers'; and at the Eucharist, as we have already seen, they are continually being recreated as angelic beings by means of Fire and Spirit (*Faith 10:9*, quoted in Chapter Six). Furthermore, spiritual wakefulness means to be single, to be in harmony, whereas if the soul is in 'sleep' it is 'divided' (*Heresies 29:35*).[9]

The ideal of wakefulness, characteristic both of the angels and of the wise virgins, together with that of singleness, would thus seem to be among the most important motivating factors that lay behind the ascetic vision and orientation of early Syriac Christianity. It was a vision which, if interiorized, Ephrem saw as being applicable to all Christians, the married just as much as the celibate, but for those who opted to live a consecrated life, as *iḥidaye* following the example of Christ the *Iḥidaya*, this vision was doubly meaningful.

Such, then, are some of the main features of the native Syrian proto-monastic tradition, of which Ephrem himself was a representative. It was a tradition quite distinct from, and independent of, Egyptian monasticism; but at the same time, since the two traditions shared many features in common, it was not difficult for the native Syrian proto-monastic tradition eventually to become absorbed into the expanding Egyptian tradition. But in Ephrem's day this had definitely not yet taken place.

9

SAINT EPHREM AMONG THE FATHERS

SAINT EPHREM AND THE GREEK FATHERS

IN THE FIRST CHAPTER I emphasized the comparatively unhellenized nature of Ephrem's thought and writings, stressing that in him we have a characteristically Semitic presentation of a Semitic religion. Although this is indeed an extremely important aspect, we should not go on to make the mistake of supposing that there is some sharp divide between the Semitic presentation of Christianity and that of Ephrem's contemporaries who wrote in Greek or Latin.

In the first place one needs to recall that, by the fourth century AD, Greek and Semitic cultures had already been interacting in the Middle East for over half a millennium: no Syriac writer of Ephrem's time is going to be purely Semitic in character or totally unhellenized; nor, for that matter, will any Greek Christian writer of that time be totally unsemitized. It is simply a matter of degree.

Furthermore it is important not to regard the existence of the two poles of 'Hellenic' and 'Semitic' as implying that the difference between the two approaches is inherently a linguistic or a cultural one: the opposition should, rather, be seen as lying between a philosophical and analytical approach on the one hand, and on the other an approach that is primarily symbolic and synthetic. The former happens to be characteristic of much Greek theological writing, the latter of early Syriac authors and of the

143

Biblical texts themselves. Some of the Greek Fathers, however, (and this is by no means confined to the great liturgical poets like Romanos) at times make use of symbolic theological language in much the same way that Ephrem does, and conversely many later Syriac theologians adopt the opposite course and allow the character of their theological discussion to be dictated entirely by the concerns, frame of reference and terminology of the philosophical and analytical approach.

However one may identify these two poles, there is no doubt that they do exist, and anyone who has read both Ephrem and any of the great fourth-century Greek Christian writers cannot fail to have sensed this; yet at the same time this same reader will not fail to observe how very close, at a profounder level, Ephrem nevertheless is to his Greek contemporaries. What separates them is, not so much a basically different understanding of the central doctrines of Christianity, but rather their very different mode of presenting these doctrines.

The two approaches, philosophical and symbolic, complement rather than contradict each other. It is thus most regrettable that standard texts books on church history and doctrine usually confine their attention to the former tradition of conducting theology, as exemplified by most Greek writers of the time, and neglect the latter tradition which is to be found above all in Syriac writers of the fourth century;[1] by so doing they provide a very one-sided presentation of the fulness of fourth-century Christianity. This one-sidedness is all the more unfortunate in a modern context where the two main features that shape the Christian Greek presentation—classical Greek philosophical tradition and language, and Greek rhetoric—are of little concern or interest to Christians who come from outside the European cultural tradition. This is an aspect to which we shall be returning in the next chapter; the aim of the present chapter, however, is to indicate how close, at a fundamental level, Ephrem is to what we nowadays see as mainstream Christianity in the Greek East. He is definitely not just a freak who mysteriously emerges from some remote cultural backwater.

SAINT EPHREM AND THE CAPPADOCIAN FATHERS

In the sixth-century Life of Saint Ephrem we are told how the saint travelled to Caesarea in Cappadocia to meet Saint Basil. Ephrem arrives for the feast of Epiphany and when he first sets eyes on Saint Basil, robed in sumptuous vestments in the church, he is put off and offended; it is only when Basil starts to preach that Ephrem recognizes him to be the pillar of fire he had seen previously in a vision, for as Basil preached Ephrem beheld the Holy Spirit proceed from his mouth in the form of a dove. This encounter between Saint Ephrem and Saint Basil happens to be without any historical foundation, and it originated from a misunderstanding of some words in Saint Basil's works where he quotes an unnamed Syrian exegete as the authority for a particular interpretation. Later tradition could not resist the temptation to identify this unnamed Syrian with Saint Ephrem, even though the interpretations in question in fact conflict with what Ephrem himself has to say on the subject.[2]

Although the meeting between the two saints is historically untrue, on a deeper symbolic level it does happen to express an important truth: underneath the external differences of presentation —in the story, symbolized by Basil's off-putting rich vestments— Ephrem and the Cappadocian Fathers (of whom Basil should here simply be seen as the representative) have a great deal in common in their fundamental interests and concerns. A few examples can serve to illustrate this point; as it happens they are all taken from Saint Gregory of Nyssa, who would appear to be the closest of the Cappadocians to Saint Ephrem at this deep level of understanding.

We have seen on many occasions the fundamental importance which Ephrem attaches to the ontological chasm between Creator and created: God can only be spoken of in so far as he has revealed himself by crossing this chasm first. The reverse movement across the chasm is not possible: any human attempt to describe God's Being and the eternal generation of the Son is not only impossible but blasphemous as well. God's Being belongs to an area of hiddenness and silence. Put in somewhat different terms, this is exactly the message of Gregory of Nyssa in his

Commentary on Ecclesiastes 3:7, "A time to keep silence and a time to speak":[3]

> In speaking of God, when there is a question of His Essence (or Being), then 'is the time to keep silence'. When, however, it is a question of His operation, a knowledge of which can come down even to us, that is the time to speak of His omnipotence by telling of His works and explaining His deeds, and to use words to this extent. In matters that go beyond this, however, the creature must not exceed the bounds of its nature, but must be content to know itself. And indeed . . . if the creature never comes to know itself, never understands the nature of the body, the cause of being, . . . how can it ever explain things which are beyond it?[4]

Another intriguing point of contact (not of course direct) between Ephrem and the Cappadocian Fathers lies in their common interest in the 'names' of God. For all these Fathers, as for the author of the dionysian corpus later, the divine names constitute one of the main modes of God's self-revelation to humanity. Gregory of Nyssa, like Ephrem, stresses that they are given purely out of God's condescension.[5] They also serve as a veil to hide the overpowering brightness of the Godhead: God descends to speak to humanity on its own level, and Gregory even talks of God 'putting on anger' in very much the same way as does Ephrem. The following excerpt, from Gregory's work against Eunomios (II.417–9) could almost (apart from some of the phraseology) be mistaken for something in Ephrem:

> Just as the sun mingles the violence of its naked rays with the air in order to bring light and warmth commensurate with those who receive it, being in itself unapproachable by our weak nature, so too does the divine Might . . . like a mother full of compassion, . . . ordain for human nature only what it is capable of receiving. For this reason it fashions itself after the manner of human beings in various revelations, and it speaks as a human being, clothing itself in anger and mercy and

other such passions; so that by thus accommodating itself to us, it may take our infant state by the hand and
lead it up through the words of Providence to touch
the nature of God.

A little over a century later the unknown author of the Dionysian
writings certainly will have drawn upon the Cappadocians as well
as upon the Neoplatonist philosopher Proclus when he wrote
his famous treatise on the Divine Names. Could it be that this
most hellenized of all Christian writers also owes something to
the Semitic Ephrem, as far as his theology of names is concerned?
This is certainly a topic worth investigating, and should there prove
to be anything in the suggestion, then we would have further evidence for the Syrian and Syriac background of that mysterious
author.[6] In any case it can be said that Ephrem has the distinction
of being one of the earliest Christian writers to have developed
such a 'theology of names'.

One can also observe that Ephrem and Gregory have many
individual themes and points of emphasis in common; thus, for
example:
—both writers stress the fundamental importance of human freedom and free will: *ḥerutha* in Ephrem, *proairesis* and *autexousiotes*
in Gregory;
—both regularly employ light imagery, and here it may be noted
that Ephrem's concept of 'hiddenness' corresponds functionally
to that of *gnophos* in Gregory, the divine darkness caused by the
superabundance of light;
—both make abundant use of mirror imagery, in particular in
connection with their descriptions of how the vision of the inner
eye of faith functions;
—both have a fundamentally sacramental understanding of the
world and a dynamic concept of salvation;
—both make considerable use of the imagery of Christ as the
heavenly Bridegroom;[7]
—both suggest that it is the awareness of separation from God that
constitutes the real torture of Gehenna.

It is at the level of the deep structures of their theological vision that Ephrem and the Cappadocian Fathers would appear to have much in common; and it is only when one turns to the surface structures that obvious differences begin to stand out—differences chiefly due to the fact that Ephrem is not writing in the philosophical and rhetorical tradition that characterizes the work of the Cappadocian Fathers.

Enough has been said, I hope, to indicate that comparative studies of Ephrem and the Cappadocians (and in particular Gregory of Nyssa) would be well worth undertaking. Indeed they could well shed a new perspective on our understanding of these Fathers' relationship to contemporary schools of thought. Thus, when Gregory of Nyssa makes use of the antinomies of moral beauty and ugliness, we should not at once, having passages such as Plotinus' *Enneads* I.6 in mind, suppose that he is necessarily writing under Neoplatonist influence, for Ephrem also happens to be extremely fond of the same antithesis: clearly this sort of imagery is part of the general religious language of the time, and was not confined to any one specific school of thought.

DIVINIZATION (*THEOSIS*)

There is one feature in particular of Ephrem's spiritual world vision which excellently illustrates how close he is, when it comes to fundamentals, to some of the great theologians of the Greek-speaking Church. Although their manner and mode of expression is often far apart, yet the basic content of what they are saying is essentially the same.

As is well known to students of church history and doctrine, the great German scholar Adolf von Harnack saw a process of corruption of the primitive Gospel message as it became more and more hellenized. What perhaps shocked von Harnack—and others—most of all was the concept of *theosis*, the divinization of humanity, a doctrine which is already found in several fourth-century Greek writers, but which was to become especially prominent in some later Greek theologians, such as Dionysius the Areopagite and Maximus the Confessor. It may thus come as something of a surprise to find that the basic features of this allegedly 'hellenistic' doctrine are already to be found in one of the least hellenized of all early Christian writers, Ephrem.

We have in fact already met this theme in passing, in an earlier chapter, while tracing the role of the 'robe of glory' over the entire span of salvation history. We saw that Adam and Eve had been created in an intermediate state, a consequence of their having been created with free will. In his *Commentary on Genesis* (*II.23*) Ephrem explains what would have happened if they had chosen to obey God's commandment:

> . . . had the serpent been rejected, along with sin, they would have eaten of the Tree of Life, and the Tree of Knowledge would no longer have been withheld from them. From the latter they would have acquired infallible knowledge, while from the former they would have received immortal life. They would have acquired divinity in humanity. And had they thus acquired infallible knowledge and immortal life, they would have done so in this body.

It was of course divinity that the serpent misleadingly promised Eve. In the event it was her desire to try to seize divinity by ignoring the divine command that led to her losing this divinity altogether. Ephrem's comments at this point are worth quoting at some length:

> She could very well have said to the serpent: 'If I cannot see (as you claim), how is it that I see everything that is to be seen? And if I do not know the difference between good and evil (as you imply), how could I discern whether your counsel is good or evil? How would I know that divinity is good, and the opening of the eyes an excellent thing, and whence would I recognize that death is evil? But all this is available to me, so why have you come to me? Your coming to us bears witness that we actually possess these very things: for with the sight that I have, and with the ability to

distinguish what is good from what is evil that I possess,
I will test your counsel. If I already have the things that
you have promised, where is all this cunning of yours
which has failed to hide your deception?'

But she did not say these things whereby she might
have defeated the serpent; but instead she fixed her eyes
on the Tree, thereby hastening her own defeat. Thus,
following her desire and enticed by the divinity which
the serpent had promised her, she ate furtively, away
from her husband. Only subsequently did she give it
to her husband, and he ate with her. Because she had
believed the serpent, she ate first, imagining that she
would return clothed in divinity to her husband whom
she had left while still a woman. She hastily ate before
her husband so that she might become head over her
head, and that she might be giving orders to him from
whom she received orders, seeing that she would have
become senior in divinity to Adam to whom she was
junior in humanity.

(*Commentary on Genesis II.20*)

The Paradise Hymns (12:15–18) paint a similar picture:

Two trees did God place in Paradise,
the Tree of Life and that of Wisdom,
a pair of blessed fountains, source of every good.
By means of this glorious pair
the human person can become the likeness of God,
endowed with immortal life and wisdom that does not
    err.

In the case of that manifest knowledge which God gave
    to Adam,
through which he gave names to Eve and to the ani-
    mals,
God did not reveal its further properties, the knowledge
    of hidden things;

that hidden knowledge
extends far beyond the stars: Adam was only able to attain
to an enquiry of all that is within this universe.

For God would not grant him the crown without some
  effort:
He placed two crowns for Adam, for which he was to
  strive,
two trees to provide crowns if he were victorious.
If only he had conquered just for one moment
he would have eaten of the one tree and lived, eaten
  of the other and gained knowledge—
a life protected from harm, a wisdom that could not
  go astray . . .

The Just One did not wish to give Adam the crown
  for nothing,
even though He had allowed him to enjoy Paradise
  without toil;
God knew that if Adam wanted he could win the prize.
It was because the Just One wished to enhance him:
for although the rank of supernal beings is great
  through grace,
the crown for the proper use of human free will is no
  small thing either.

The effect of eating of the Tree of Knowledge turns out to depend
entirely on the attitude of the eater: the knowledge gained is in
itself neutral, but how it is experienced is another matter: where
acquired in arrogance and greed, the knowledge will prove bitter
and even harmful; only in the context of obedience to the divine
command will it be beneficial. Ephrem dwells on this double-
edged characteristic of the Tree of Knowledge especially in the
third of the Paradise Hymns (3:8):

Whoever has eaten of that fruit is granted a perception
which either delights him or fills him with abhorrence.

> The serpent incited them to eat in sin, so that they
>   might sorrow:
> although they had glimpsed the blessed state, they could
>   not partake of it.
> Like that hero of old (Tantalus), whose torment was
>   doubled
> because, although ravenous, he could not taste the de-
>   lights he beheld.

Thus, according to Ephrem, it is precisely because humanity
grabbed at divinity out of arrogance that humanity lost the reward
of divinity which God had intended if free will had properly been
exercised. So great, however, is God's love for humanity that, not
only does he endeavour to bring Adam/humanity back to Paradise,
but, as Ephrem puts it in one of the *Nisibene Hymns* (*69:12*):[8]

> The Most High knew that Adam had wanted to be-
>   come a god,
> so He sent His Son who put him on in order to grant
>   him his desire.

Yet again we can see the very close associations in Ephrem's
mind between First Adam, Christ the Second Adam, and humanity; the First Adam belongs to primordial time, the Second Adam,
or the 'God-Human' as Ephrem twice describes him,[9] belongs to
historical time, while humanity's destined potential of divinity belongs to the eschaton.

The concept of divinization in Ephrem is a natural outcome of
the pattern of complementarity which he sees between the divine
descent and its purpose, namely the restoration of Adam and the
human ascent. The same pattern that we found in the Nisibene
Hymn recurs in one of the Hymns on Virginity (48:15–18):

> Free will succeeded in making Adam's beauty ugly,
> for he, a man, sought to become a god.
>
> Grace, however, made beautiful his deformities
> and God came to become a man.

Divinity flew down
to draw humanity up,

For the Son had made beautiful the deformities of the
    servant
and so he has become a god, just as he desired.

The raising up of Adam/humanity to a higher level in the
eschatological Paradise is also touched on in one of the Paradise
Hymns. In this hymn cycle Ephrem gives various analogies to the
different levels of the Paradise mountain: the different storeys in
Noah's Ark (Noah and his family, the birds, the animals), the
various levels on Mount Sinai (Moses, Aaron, the people), the
different parts of the Sanctuary (Holy of Holies, the Veil, the Holy
Place), and finally, the tripartite nature of humanity, consisting of
intellectual spirit (*tar'itha*), soul (*naphsha*) and body (*gushma*). In
the eschatological paradise each of these, spirit, soul, body, will
be raised one step higher:

Far more glorious than the body is the soul,
and more glorious still than the soul is the spirit,
but more hidden than the spirit is the Godhead.
At the end, the body will put on
the beauty of the soul, the soul will put on that of the
    spirit,
while the spirit will put on the very likeness of God's
    majesty.

(*Paradise 9:20*)[10]

We should not, however, misunderstand Ephrem and suppose
either that he envisages a merging of humanity into the Godhead,
or that divinized humanity will in any way be on a par with God.
Ephrem is very much aware that divinized humanity will have
achieved this status solely through grace: the First Adam becomes
a god by grace, whereas the Second Adam is God by nature: as
Ephrem puts it:

God in his mercy called mortals 'gods through grace'.

(*Faith 29:1*)

Theosis is thus to be seen as part of the 'exchange of names'. The ontological gap, however, between Creator and created is fully preserved: as Ephrem once expressed the matter, God had created Adam with the potential of being a 'created god'.[11] What characterizes the divinity that has been made available for humanity is, according to Ephrem, the possession of immortality and infallible knowledge.[12] The doctrine of *theosis* or divinization, as Ephrem understands it, is just a way of making explicit what it means to become 'children of God', seeing that in the Semitic languages the term *bar*, 'son of', may have the sense of 'sharing in the attributes of' or 'belonging to the category of'.

In Ephrem's hands the doctrine of *theosis* is by no means an outcome of 'the poison of the pagan Greeks'; rather, it turns out to be firmly rooted in his exegesis of the Paradise narrative and in his understanding of the whole aim and purpose of the Incarnation.

The juxtaposition of two epigrammatic expressions of this doctrine will provide an appropriate conclusion to our discussion of this topic. The first is well known and comes from Saint Athanasius: 'God became man so that man might become god'; the second, from Saint Ephrem's Hymns on Faith (5:17) is hardly any different in basic content:

> He gave us divinity,
> we gave Him humanity.

SAINT EPHREM AND LATER MONASTIC TRADITION

In Chapter Eight it was pointed out that the standard later depiction of Saint Ephrem as a monk of strictest asceticism was anachronistic: he cannot have been a monk in the formal sense of the term, and he would only have become aware of the spread of Egyptian monasticism in the latter part of his life. Instead, Ephrem belonged to the native Syrian ascetic tradition, to what I have called proto-monasticism; in all probability he was himself an *ihidaya*.[13] This proto-monasticism indeed also involved a consecrated life of virginity and celibacy, and those who lived it seem to have lived in small communal groups; but two things in particular distinguished them from Egyptian monasticism: these groups were essentially informal in character and had nothing of the structured life characteristic of cenobitic monasticism; and secondly, they lived within towns and villages, and not outside them: with the exception perhaps of a few individuals, there was no question yet of anachoresis, the physical withdrawal from ordinary life.

So Ephrem stands apart from later monasticism, just as his theological approach stands apart from that of his Greek contemporaries. Yet at the same time, just as Ephrem is, at a fundamental level, nevertheless in very close agreement with his Greek contemporaries, so too is he very close in spirit to the nascent monastic movement, even though formally we need to disassociate him from it.

It was in fact precisely because later monastic circles saw him as a kindred spirit that they depicted him as a monk: the process begins already with Palladius, writing about half a century after Ephrem's death, for he includes a chapter on Saint Ephrem in his Lausiac History and speaks of his cell. As time goes on the biographical tradition depicts Ephrem more and more in the role of a monk, and in due course, in the sixth-century Life, he is even accredited with a visit to Egypt and a meeting with Anba Bishoi (Pisoes). The memory of this supposed visit is still very much alive in the monasteries of the Wadi Natroun in modern Egypt today.

We should regard this supposed visit of Ephrem to the monasteries of Egypt in the same light as his visit to Saint Basil: neither visit has any historical foundation, but both express a certain truth at a symbolic level.

Ephrem's links with monasticism, as they were perceived by later generations, could be said to have borne fruit in two different ways. First, sayings attributed to him feature in the monastic collections of apophthegmata (the early Syriac translator of Palladius' Lausiac History has already inserted a couple of these into Palladius' brief section on Ephrem). Secondly (and this is of far greater importance), Ephrem's works became a source of inspiration for later writers on monastic spirituality,[14] and many of the themes which he had already developed in his hymns became central in later monastic literature. A few examples will serve to illustrate this point.

We saw in Chapter Seven something of Ephrem's predilection for bridal imagery, with Christ the Bridegroom and the Church or the individual soul as the bride. Anyone who has read the Macarian Homilies will know how popular there the theme of Christ 'the heavenly Bridegroom' is. The Macarian Homilies of course have a Syrian or Mesopotamian background, and will have come from monastic communities which were probably as much indebted to the native Syrian proto-monastic tradition to which Saint Ephrem belonged, as they were to Egyptian monasticism.

We have also had occasion to observe the importance of the terms *shaphya, shaphyutha*, 'luminous, luminosity' etc.[15] These were to become key terms in the great East Syrian writers on the spiritual life in the seventh and eighth centuries, and in between them and Ephrem they had already come to feature prominently in the writings of John of Apamea and Philoxenus of Mabbugh. *Shaphya* is an adjective which is especially used to describe the state of the heart or the mind. There is another phrase connected with the heart which is also worth noticing: the later East Syrian writers frequently applied the Gospel parable of the Sower to the interior life, and so the good soil where the seed is thrown and thrives is often called 'the soil/land of the heart',[16] a phrase already found a few times in Ephrem's hymns; for example:

> Once Nature and Scripture had cleansed the land
> they sowed in it new commandments
> —in the land of the heart, so that it might bear fruit,
> praise for the Lord of Nature,
> glory for the Lord of Scripture.
>
> (*Heresies 28:11*)

Again, Ephrem frequently employs the verbs 'mix', 'mingle' in order to describe divine activity within creation, as for example:

> The Firstborn put on real limbs
> and was mingled in with humanity:
> He gave what belongs to Him
> and took what belongs to us,

so that His mingling
might give life to our mortal state.

(Heresies 32:9)

Although this sort of language later fell out of favour in a strictly Christological context, it nevertheless remained a central way of describing the interaction between human and divine in almost all later Syriac writers on the spiritual life, from John of Apamea onwards.

A final example of the close links in thought between Ephrem and later Syriac monastic writers is provided by the parallelism which they all see between the Incarnation and the Eucharistic Epiclesis: Mary's conception and birth-giving serves as the model for the interiorized conception and birth-giving that individual Christians may experience as a result of the 'overshadowing' of the Holy Spirit.[17]

The paradoxes that have emerged in the course of this chapter—Ephrem's closeness at an interior level both to his contemporaries among the Greek Fathers and to subsequent monastic tradition, despite his marked exterior distance from them all—will not be seen as inappropriate, applying as they do to this poet par excellence of the paradox.

10

SAINT EPHREM TODAY

IN 1920 SAINT EPHREM was proclaimed by Pope Benedict XV to be a Doctor of the Church. It would be interesting to know what had led Pope Benedict to make the declaration at that particular time when there were only imperfect and incomplete editions of his works available, and very few translations into modern European languages. Today, now that we have Dom Edmund Beck's fine edition of the great hymn cycles, we are in a far better position to appreciate the wisdom of that proclamation.

In this final chapter we shall consider five areas where it would seem that Saint Ephrem has important things to say which are of particular relevance to our condition today.[1] Since most of these are areas which have already been touched upon in earlier chapters, it will sometimes only be necessary to recapitulate what has been said earlier.

EPHREM AS A REPRESENTATIVE OF ASIAN CHRISTIANITY

Christianity was born in a Semitic milieu, a milieu that was specifically Aramaic speaking, but since the Gospels were written down in Greek, Greek rapidly became the main literary language of early Christianity, and consequently in the course of time theological language and method became thoroughly hellenized.

It is, of course, in this hellenized form of Christianity that European Christianity, in its many different manifestations today, has its roots.

Although early Syriac Christianity received the written Gospels,[2] not directly from Palestinian Aramaic, but by way of translations from Greek, it was not until the fifth century onwards that Syriac Christianity really adopted Greek thought forms and itself became strongly hellenized, with the result that Syriac theology of the early middle ages was as much influenced by Aristotle as was Latin: both Syriac and Latin were heirs of the same educational system that obtained in the sixth-century Christian schools of the Greek East.[3] The course of theological discussion was by then dictated entirely by Greek concerns and terminology even when it was conducted in other languages.

Ephrem, however, belongs to a period when the theological terms of reference were still primarily Syriac, and when Syriac Christianity was as yet comparatively little touched by this process of hellenization, or as we may call it, Europeanization or Westernization. He represents a genuinely Semitic form of Christianity, and thus a genuinely Asian form of Christianity. He is then a writer who very much deserves the attention of all those today in Asia and Africa, and elsewhere, who are looking for a form of Christianity that is not burdened by European intellectual and cultural trappings.

POETRY AS A VEHICLE FOR THEOLOGY

Ephrem is a theologian who employs poetry as the principal vehicle of his theology. Because of the way in which the study of theology has grown up in the West we have all too often forgotten that poetry can prove to be an excellent medium for creative theological writing. Because the theologian poet is using a literary form that instinctively shrinks back from any attempt to encapsulate eternal verities and truths in fixed formulae and dogmatic definitions, he is able to present an essentially dynamic theological vision, continually urging the reader to move on beyond the outer garment of words to the inner meaning and truth to which they point:

It is not at the clothing of the words
that one should gaze,
but at the power hidden in the words.

(*Church 28:17*)

As a consequence Ephrem's writings still retain a great freshness and immediacy for the modern reader, all the moreso seeing
that his profound and powerful theological vision is not described
within the framework of a particular European or Western philosophical tradition; rather, he presents it by means of images that are
drawn both from the Bible and from perennial human experience,
eating and drinking, dressing and undressing, birth and death, thus
lending to his poetry a timeless character. Furthermore, the Syriac poetic medium through which Ephrem works has the added
advantage of being completely free from the somewhat deadening literary conventions of the Graeco-Latin rhetorical tradition
of late antiquity, conventions that can often seem tiresome to the
modern reader.

THE INTERPRETATION OF SCRIPTURE
WITHIN THE CONTEXT OF FAITH

The third area where Saint Ephrem seems to be saying something that is still of fundamental value stems from his essentially
sacramental approach to both Scripture and the world of nature
around us. Needless to say, Ephrem's method of scriptural exegesis will have no appeal to the modern biblical scholar, whose
primary concern is with historical truth; this is because Ephrem
is interested in a very different mode of understanding, where
the object of enquiry is not historical truth but spiritual reality
—a different sort of truth, possessing a different mode of
objectivity.

Both approaches are equally valid, and provided that neither
side makes exclusive claims, they can happily, and indeed fruitfully,
co-exist.[4] Ephrem's concern is almost exclusively with the second
approach, the search for spiritual reality, which he simply calls
'truth'. This approach operates solely from the starting point of
faith, and provided we remember this, Ephrem's understanding of

how this approach can operate has just as great a relevance today as it did in the fourth century.[5]

The basic structure of Ephrem's understanding of the interpretation of Scripture may be summarized along the following lines. Scripture possesses two kinds of meaning, the outer historical meaning, and the inner spiritual meaning, 'the hidden power' as Ephrem sometimes calls it. These two coexist as intimately as do the humanity and the divinity in the incarnate Christ. Ephrem's belief in the presence of the 'hidden power' could be said to correspond to the traditional doctrine of the divine inspiration of the Scriptures.

The inner meaning, or 'hidden power', is as objectively present in Scripture as is the outer historical meaning. But whether its presence is actually perceived by the reader or hearer of Scripture is another matter, for this inner meaning can only be perceived by the inner eye, and the light by which that eye operates is the light of faith. That light is always available, but the individual inner eye can at will shut this out, or dim it. Whether a person makes any use of this inner mode of vision in the first place, and then, the extent to which she or he does so, is thus ultimately a matter of free choice, the exercise of free will. Put in different terms, the extent to which an individual can see with this inner eye will depend on the extent to which he or she is open to the continuing inspiration of the Holy Spirit. To appreciate the inspiration of the biblical text the reader must himself be open to the inspiration of the Spirit.

Symbols and types play a central role. Some idea of how these operate for Ephrem can be illustrated by an analogy. Scripture could be described as a darkened plate of glass between humanity and divine reality (Ephrem's 'truth'). The outer meanings correspond to what can be seen on the surface of the glass: this is the object of enquiry for biblical scholarship. But on this surface are a whole number of pinpoints of varying size, where the glass is clear, thus giving the possibility of vision through and beyond the glass itself. These pinpoints correspond to Ephrem's *raze*, symbols and types. Their very presence on the glass is, in the first place, only visible to the inner eye which sees by the light of faith. But given that the inner eye does perceive them, then two rather different things will affect the vision of this eye: it may be obscured by sin or distorted by wrong belief (both very important points for Ephrem), and, secondly, any strength it has will depend on the strength of its faith. The greater the faith, the closer to the glass will the inner eye get, with a twofold result: in the first place it will see yet more pinpoints, that is *raze* or symbols, on the glass through which to look beyond to 'truth'; and secondly, the eye will get a much wider vision of truth the closer it gets to the glass. This helps to explain why *raze* or symbols are multivalent; to say that a symbol can point to only one thing, has only one interpretation, is to misunderstand what these symbols are all about.

Ephrem shares with us some of his excitement at what he beholds with his inner eye of faith in one of the Paradise Hymns (5:3–4):

> I read the opening of this book★   ★*Genesis*
> and was filled with joy,
> for its verses and lines
> spread out their arms to welcome me;
> the first rushed out and kissed me,
> and led me on to its companions.
> And when I reached that line
> where the story
> of Paradise is written, it lifted me up
> and transported me
> from the bosom of the Book
> to the very bosom of Paradise.
>
> The eye and the mind
> travelled over the lines
> as over a bridge, and entered all at once
> the tale of Paradise.
> In its reading the eye had
> transported the mind,
> in return the mind too
> let the eye rest

from its reading,
for when the Book had been read
the eye had rest
but the mind was engaged.

The analogy of Scripture as a darkened glass in fact serves just as well to illustrate Ephrem's understanding of the role of symbols in nature. It is to this natural world of creation that we next turn, but here we shall be looking at Ephrem's contribution from a rather different point of view.

EPHREM'S ECOLOGICAL VISION

The fourth area where Ephrem would appear to have contemporary interest concerns the awareness he has of the interconnectedness of everything. Nothing in creation exists in isolation. The relationship of humanity to nature, and the attitude of mankind to the environment and his use of it, are matters of profound significance for Ephrem. he would make an appropriate patron saint for ecologically-minded people.

As we have had occasion to observe many times, Nature, the natural world, stands side by side with Scripture as a witness to God:

In his book Moses described
the creation of the natural world,
so that both the natural world and His book
might testify to the Creator:
the natural world, through humanity's use of it,
the book, through his reading of it.

(*Paradise* 5:2)

It is humanity's attitude to, and use of, the natural world around us that is of fundamental importance, and these are both factors which are governed by the right exercise of free will. The responsibility for a right response lies with the individual human person. For Ephrem the right response is essentially one of wonder and gratitude, whereas the wrong response will be made wherever greed and arrogance are present. The right response, moreover, will always be coupled with an awareness that inherent in the natural world (as in Scripture) are these innumerable symbols that the inner eye of faith can use as vehicles conveying its vision to the world of spiritual reality. The presence of this 'hidden power' in the natural world lends to the natural world itself a sacramental character, which in turn requires that the natural world be used with reverence.

Moral evil on man's part, the misuse of his free will, disturbs the cosmic harmony and order. As Ephrem sees it, the ill effects on the natural order, brought about by human misuse of the divine gift of free will, can already be observed in the paradigmatic account of Paradise and the Fall:

> The sprouting of the thorn (Gen. 3:18)
> testified to the novel sprouting of wrong actions,
> for thorns did not sprout
> as long as wrong-doing had not yet burst forth;
> but once there had peered out
> hidden wrong choices made by free will,
> then the visible thorns began to peer out from the earth.
>
> (*Heresies 28:9*)

And in his Commentary on Genesis (II.31) Ephrem specifically states that, had there been no sin, the earth would never have brought forth the thorns. Likewise wild animals prove harmful to human beings only *after* the Fall: in Paradise they had lived in harmony with Adam and Eve—a harmony that will be recovered in the eschatological Paradise, and occasionally anticipated on earth by the saints.[6]

Human injustice has consequences that go far beyond the immediate context of that injustice; Ephrem expresses this by taking a biblical example, the case of queen Jezebel (1 Kings 21):

> Because Jezebel defrauded Truth,
> the earth refused its produce,
> the womb of the earth held back, as a reproof,
> the seeds that the farmer had lent it:

the earth suffocated the seeds within itself
because its inhabitants had deceitfully held back truth.
(*Virginity 7:3*)

And, commenting on Matthew 27:51, 'And the mountains shook, graves were opened and the veil was torn' (at the time of the Crucifixion), Ephrem writes;

Because the mouth of human beings had condemned
Him, the voice of creation cried out to proclaim Him
innocent. Men were silent, so the stones cried out.
(*Commentary on the Diatessaron* 21:5)

Paradoxically, the far-flung consequences of human injustice may themselves provide the possibility for restoration. The crucified Christ himself offers the means for forgiveness for the very people who had crucified him:

. . . they pierced You with the sword, and there sprung
   forth water
—for the wiping away of their sins.
(*Virginity 30:10*)

The same principle applies in all sorts of other contexts as well:

One person falls sick—and so another can visit and
   help him;
one person starves—and so another can provide him
   with food and give him life;
one person does something stupid—
but he can be instructed by another and thereby grow.
In this way the world can recover:
tens of thousands of hidden ways are to be found,
ready to assist us.
(*Heresies 10:9*)

It is the exercise of human justice that lends harmony both to society and to creation as a whole, whereas injustice upsets this harmony. Although the original state of harmony has manifestly been lost as a result of the abuse of human free will, nevertheless the potential for recovery is always present through right choices and through the right use of creation. Just as a body only functions harmoniously if all the different limbs cooperate, so too humanity as a whole will only achieve a harmonious world society if each helps fill in the needs of others:

> For just as in the case of the limbs of the body, their individual needs are fulfilled by one another, so too the inhabitants of the world fill in the common need from the common excess. We should rejoice in this need on the part of us all, for out of it is born harmony for us all; for in that people need one another, those in high position stoop to the lowly and are not ashamed, and the insignificant reach out to the powerful and are not afraid. Even in the case of animals, seeing that we have a need for them, we take care of them. Clearly our need for everything binds us with a love for everything.
>
> (*Letter to Hypatius*, ed. Overbeck, p. 26)

In modern terms one could say that for Ephrem the physical and spiritual ecospheres are intimately linked: because of the interconnectedness between everything, the abuse of nature, resulting from the human misuse of free will, will have consequences in all sorts of unexpected places.

It is truly remarkable that in all this Ephrem often appears to be pointing in very much the same direction as some exponents of modern scientific thinking. These trends are well described for the lay reader by Fritjof Capra in his important book *The Turning Point* (1982): Capra takes as his starting point the revolution in our understanding of the nature of the universe brought about by advances this century in sub-atomic physics. No longer is the universe seen as some sort of machine composed of a multitude of separate objects; rather it 'has to be pictured as one indivisible, dynamic whole whose parts are essentially interrelated and can be understood only as patterns of a cosmic process', where 'the behavior of any part is determined by its non-local connections to the whole'.[7] Capra goes on to extend this new scientific awareness of the interrelatedness and interdependence of everything to

other spheres, such as biology, medicine, psychology and eco-
nomics. This 'systems view of life', as he calls it, turns out to
be astonishingly consonant (*mutatis mutandis*) with Ephrem's own
perceptions.[8] But perhaps this should not really surprise us, for,
as Capra himself points out, the themes of 'the universal interconnectedness and interdependence of all phenomena, and the
intrinsically dynamic nature of reality' are recurrent in the mystical thought of many different religious traditions.[9]

<h3 style="text-align:center">THE ROLE OF THE FEMININE</h3>

The fifth area of special interest that Ephrem's writings have for
the modern world concerns the role he accords to the feminine in
theology. This is of course a topic that has been unduly neglected
in the past, but which has now come to forefront, notably in
the United States of America. Ephrem happens to have much
of interest and value to contribute on the subject, and here we
shall briefly glance at three different aspects: the fact that many of
Ephrem's hymns were written specifically for women's choirs; his
interest in, and sensitivity for, women who feature in the Bible;
and his very extensive use of feminine imagery in his poetry.

The Syriac poet Jacob of Serugh, who died in 521, has a poem
on Saint Ephrem where he dwells on the fact that Ephrem was an
author who wrote specifically for women:[10]

> The wise Moses caused the virgins
> not to hold back from the praise that was requisite;
> so too Ephrem, who proved a second Moses to women
> folk,
> taught them to sing praise with the sweetest of songs.

And a little further on:[11]

> The blessed Ephrem saw that the women were silent
> from praise
> and in his wisdom he decided it was right that they
> should sing out;
> so, just as Moses gave timbrels to the young girls,
> thus did this discerning man compose hymns for vir-
> gins.

As he stood among the sisters it was his delight
to stir these chaste women into songs of praise;
he was like an eagle perched among the doves
as he taught them to sing new songs of praise with pure
    utterance.
Flocks of meek partridge surrounded him,
learning how to sing a sweet song with purity of voice.
He taught the swallows to warble
and the Church resounded with the lovely sound of
    chaste women's voices.

When we consider how little is heard about the role of women
in liturgical worship in the early Church, Ephrem's activities in
writing hymns for them to sing become all the more remarkable.

That Ephrem had great feeling for women comes over clearly
in both his poetry and prose from the way in which he handles
biblical themes involving women, as well as from the frequency
with which he introduces them. A few examples must suffice to
illustrate this.

In the Commentary on Genesis XX.1 Ephrem (like many other
contemporary commentators) wonders why Abraham apparently
did not say anything to his wife Sarah when he took Isaac off to
sacrifice him in obedience to God's command. He did not tell
her because he had not been told to tell her, explains Ephrem;
but then he adds: 'had he told her, she would have begged to
come and share in the sacrifice just as Abraham had made her
share in the promise of Isaac's birth'. In other words, her faith in
God, and her love of God, was just as great as Abraham's. Just
how remarkable Ephrem's comment here is, best stands out when
one compares it with the standard exegetical tradition, which is
often blatantly anti-feminist on this point. It is worth mention-
ing in passing that Ephrem's very positive attitude to Sarah is
developed further in an anonymous fifth-century poem on the
sacrifice of Isaac, and probably from thence it was picked up in
the second half of the *kontakion*, or hymn, on the same subject
by Romanos, the sixth-century Greek poet from Emesa (Homs)
in Syria.[12]

Another example is provided by Ephrem's comments on the episode of Rachel stealing the gods (that is, idols) of her father Laban, and going off with Jacob (Genesis 31). On the surface this might look like a rather compromising incident, but not so for Ephrem, who says:

> Now Jacob loved Rachel greatly, since she loved his God and despised her father's images: for not only by stealing them did she dishonour them as something totally useless, but she even made them into a seat for menstruation when her father's servants searched for them.
>
> (*Commentary on Genesis XXVIII.4*)

The episode of Tamar (Gen. 38) who, by a ruse, succeeded in having a child by her father-in-law Judah, is given a considerable amount of space by Ephrem (*Commentary on Genesis XXXIV*). Tamar does this, not because 'she hungered for intercourse', but because 'she yearned for the Blessing that was hidden', that is, the Messiah, whose ancestry passed through Judah.

Many further examples could be adduced, including some surprising cases like Lot's two daughters who slept with their father, and Potiphar's wife who had tried to seduce Joseph. Among the New Testament women, apart from Jesus' mother, it is the woman who anointed Jesus who particularly caught Ephrem's attention.

In the light of all this the frequency with which Ephrem makes use of feminine imagery will cause no surprise. We have in fact already many times had occasion to notice how fond Ephrem is of images of conceiving and birthgiving, of the womb and bosom. Nor is the imagery confined to the created world, for Ephrem is not afraid to apply it to the Godhead as well. Here, at the outset, we should recall the well-known fact that in early Syriac literature the Holy Spirit, *ruha d-qudsha*, is treated grammatically as a feminine. The significance of this usage should not, however, be over-emphasized, for we also need to recall that in the same early Syriac writers the divine Word, *melta*, translating Greek Logos, is also treated grammatically as a feminine. This usage is still to be found in Ephrem's writings.[13]

Perhaps of greater significance is the use Ephrem makes of the term *'ubba*, 'bosom', but also 'womb', with reference to the Father. The term derives from John 1:18, 'No one has ever seen God; the only Son, who is in the bosom of the Father, he has made him known'. The Greek text here has *kolpos*, 'bosom', but the early Syriac translators chose to render the word, not by *kenpa*, 'lap, bosom', but by *ubba*, which has a much wider range of meaning than does *kolpos*, and includes 'womb' as well as 'lap'.

In Ephrem's poetry we encounter the word *'ubba* in a great variety of different meanings, and by no means every time that he uses the word does he intend it in the sense 'womb', whether metaphorically or not. Nevertheless there remain many passages where Ephrem juxtaposes the *'ubba* of the Father with the *'ubba* of Mary, and in these it seems that we can justifiably understand the sense of 'womb' as uppermost. Thus in one of the Resurrection hymns (1:7) we have:

> The Word★ of the Father came from   ★ *feminine*
>   His womb.
> and put on a body in another womb:
> the Word proceeded from one womb to another—
> and chaste wombs are now filled with the Word:
> blessed is He who has resided in us.

The 'chaste wombs' are those of the believers; that we should translate *'ubbe* here too as 'wombs' rather than 'bosoms' is shown by Ephrem's choice of the phrase 'resided (*shra*) in us', employing a technical term which (as we saw earlier) he often uses of the 'Power of the Most High' in Mary's womb (Luke 1:35).

Other examples of feminine imagery applied to the Godhead are not hard to find; here a few further examples will suffice. The two aspects of God's activity, his Righteousness and his Grace, are both described as 'mothers' (*Church 5:1–2*), while in another hymn from the same cycle the Divinity is compared to a wet-nurse:

> The Divinity is attentive to us, just as a wetnurse is to
>   a baby,

keeping back for the right time things that will benefit
  it,
for she knows the right time for weaning,
and when the child should be nourished with milk,
and when it should be fed with solid food (*lit.* bread),
weighing out and providing what is beneficial to it
in accordance with the measure of its growing up.

(*Church 25:18*)

In a Nativity hymn, where Ephrem meditates on the paradox of the infant Christ, it is Christ himself who is 'the living breast':[14]

He was lying there, sucking Mary's milk,
yet all created things suck from His goodness.
He is the living breast: from His life
the dead have sucked living breath—and come to life.

(*Nativity 4:149–50*)

Appropriately enough there are other passages where Ephrem employs feminine imagery with reference to himself, as in the following passage already quoted in another context:

Lord, my mind is barren from giving birth to anything
  new;
grant to my mind fertility and a child, just as you did
  to Hannah,
so that the utterance of the child that shall issue from
  my mouth
may be offered up to You as was that barren woman's
  child (Samuel).

(*Church 30:1*)

CONCLUSION

There are, then, a number of good reasons why Saint Ephrem deserves, both as a poet and as a theologian, a much wider audience today than the diminutive circle of Syriac scholars. Coming from the time of the undivided Church, Ephrem belongs to the heritage of all Christian traditions. He speaks to unlearned and learned alike, to both lay and religious; and precisely because his thought and imagery are so deeply rooted in the Bible, his poetry is thereby enabled to participate in something of the perennial freshness of the biblical text itself, upon which it so often directly meditates. Not without justice has Fr. Robert Murray described him as 'the greatest poet of the patristic age, and perhaps the only theologian-poet to rank beside Dante'.[15]

It is to be hoped that, despite all the inadequacies of the presentation offered here, at least some inkling of the profundity of Ephrem's spiritual world vision will have been conveyed to the reader. Saint Ephrem is not only a poet to be read, he is also one by whom one is continually rewarded each time one re-reads him: like the types and symbols upon which he rejoices to ponder, his own poems are vehicles of an immense wealth of spiritual insight, the variety of whose treasures never ceases to give rise to astonishment in the reader who approaches them with sympathy.

A delightful paragraph on Saint Ephrem, which the Syriac translator of Palladius' Lausiac History has inserted alongside Palladius' own notice, will provide us with an suitable conclusion:[16]

> One of the holy fathers saw in a dream a band of holy angels come down from heaven at God's behest. One of them was holding in his hand a scroll written both on the inside and on the outside. They were asking each other, 'To whom should this be entrusted?' Some of them said to one particular person, and others to another; yet others, however, said 'All these people are indeed saints and upright, but they are not capable of being entrusted with it'. Having mentioned the names of many other saints, they finally said, 'No one can be entrusted with this apart from Ephrem'. Whereupon they gave it to him. When the father arose in the morning he heard people saying, 'Ephrem teaches as if a fountain was flowing from his mouth'. Then the elder who had seen the dream recognized that what issued from his lips was from the Holy Spirit.

It is said of Ephrem that when he was a boy he saw a dream, or a vision, in which a vine shoot sprang up from his tongue; it grew, and everywhere under the heaven was filled by it. It bore bunches of grapes in proliferation, and all the birds of the sky came and ate of its fruits; the more they ate, the more the bunches multiplied and grew.

NOTES

Works listed in the Select Bibliography are cited by author's name and an abbreviated form of the title only: full details will readily be found by reference to section C of the Bibliography (for books, i.e. titles in italics) and section D (for articles, i.e. titles in inverted commas).

NOTES TO CHAPTER 1

1. This process is outlined in 'From antagonism to assimilation: Syriac attitudes to Greek learning', reprinted as chapter V of my *Syriac Perspectives on Late Antiquity* (London, 1984).
2. Recorded already in Palladius' *Lausiac History*, chapter 40 (dating from 419/20).
3. The full poem is translated in my *The Harp of the Spirit*, no. 14. For this type of literature in Syriac, see 'Syriac dialogue poems: marginalia to a recent edition', *Le Muséon* 97 (1984) pp. 29–58.
4. For this aspect see for example R. Murray, *Symbols*, pp. 307–10, 338–40 and G. Widengren, *Mesopotamian Elements in Manichaeism* (Uppsala/Leipzig, 1946).
5. For this pair, see J. Martikainen, *Gerechtigkeit und Güte Gottes* (Göttingen, 1980).
6. He knows, for example, about the various views current among Greek writers on the nature of the soul (*Faith*, 1), and Beck has shown the influence of Stoic ideas in particular on Ephrem's thought (*Psychologie*, passim).

NOTES TO CHAPTER 2

1. *Faith* 69:11, quoted below.
2. The image is common in Ephrem (e.g. *Virginity* 6:9; 23:5) and other early Syriac writers, whereas among contemporary Greek and Latin writers it is rare (though in medieval art the idea came to be represented pictorially quite often).

3. This is common to all early Syriac writers; see further my 'Clothing Metaphors'.
4. For this see G. Winkler, 'The original meaning of the pre-baptismal anointing and its implications', *Worship* 52 (1978) pp. 24–45, and my 'The transition to a post-baptismal anointing in the Antiochene rite', in B.D. Spinks, ed., *The Sacrifice of Praise: Studies in Honour of A.H. Couratin. Ephemerides Liturgicae*, Subsidia 19; (1981) pp. 215–25.
5. This imagery has been studied by E. Beck, 'Das Bild vom Spiegel', and by M. Schmidt, 'Die Augensymbolik'.
6. In the version of the letter given by Eusebius (*Ecclesiastical History* I.13,6), however, Abgar addresses Christ as 'the good Saviour'.
7. Complete translations of this fine hymn on the Eucharist are available by R. Murray in *Eastern Churches Review* 3 (1970) pp. 142–50, and by S. P. Brock, *St Ephrem. A Hymn on the Eucharist* (Lancaster, 1986), and in *The Harp* [Kottayam, India] 1:1 (1987) pp. 61- 8.
8. This explains why the Fathers regularly speak of the literal interpretation of Scripture as something characteristic of the Jews.
9. For this analogy, see further Chapter Ten.

NOTES TO CHAPTER 3

1. On these, see especially R. Murray's 'The theory of symbolism'.
2. English translations of the poem can be found in R. N. Beshara, *Mary, Ship of Treasures* ([Brooklyn], 1988) pp. 89–92 (abbreviated) and in S. Brock, *Sogiatha. Syriac Dialogue Hymns*, Syrian Churches Series 11 (1987) pp. 14–20. (For details of editions see *Le Muséon* 97 [1984] pp. 42–43).
3. For this aspect see Chapter Ten.
4. *Faith* 81–5; French translation by F. Graffin in *L'Orient Syrien* 12 (1967) pp. 129–50.
5. For the elaborate structure of this hymn, see my 'The poetic artistry'.
6. In the previous stanza Ephrem explains how the Ark sailed to the four points of the compass (i.e. cross-wise).
7. Ephrem goes on to illustrate this from the case of the Jews who deny the Son.
8. That the name 'Father' is the logical starting point in Ephrem's argument here can be seen from *Faith* 52:1, where he says: The name of the Father indicates that He is a Begetter, for the name of fatherhood testifies concerning His Son.
9. See Chapter Nine.

NOTES TO CHAPTER 4

1. *Faith* 44:10.
2. The term is a favourite one of Ephrem's, e.g. *Faith* 32:9, *Nisibis* 49:3, *Nativity* 2:9, *Heresies* 21:8.
3. The contrast is brought out at some length in the *Commentary on the Diatessaron* 1:10- 17.

4. Luke 8:15.
5. Later in the letter (22), Ephrem speculates that Gehenna is really self-awareness of one's own sins and the consequent sense of separation from God.
6. On the exegesis of this verse in the early Syriac Fathers see R. Murray, 'The lance which re-opened Paradise', and my 'The Mysteries hidden in the side of Christ'.
7. Compare *Epiphany* 12:5.
8. On Christ as the Rock, see Murray, *Symbols*, pp. 205–12; compare *Epiphany* 5:12–14.
9. E.g. Bedjan II, p. 589:

> Christ slept on the Cross, and baptism came forth from Him; the Bridegroom slept, and His side was pierced in His sleep, He gave birth to the Bride, as happened with Eve in Adam His type. The stillness of sleep of death fell upon Him on the Cross and from Him came forth the Mother who gives birth to all spiritual beings.

A similar passage can be found in Jacob's famous homily on the Veil of Moses, translated in *Sobornost/ECR* 3:1 (1981) pp. 80–81.
10. Romanos is probably alluding to this passage in his third *kontakion* on the Resurrection (stanza 5).

NOTES TO CHAPTER 5

1. For further details, see my 'Clothing metaphors', and 'Some aspects of Greek words in Syriac', reprinted in *Syriac Perspective on Late Antiquity*, Chapter IV, pp. 98–104.
2. A complete translation of the poem is given in *Eastern Churches Review* 7 (1976) pp. 137–44. For stanza Six compare *Virginity* 32:5.
3. E.g. *Discourse on our Lord*, 1; cp E. Beck, 'Das Bild vom Weg mit Meilensteinen'.
4. Ed. Bedjan, III: p. 593.
5. On this, see especially H. J. W. Drijvers and G. J. Reinink, 'Taufe und Licht: Tatian, Ebionäerevangelium und Thomasakten', in *Text and Testimony. Essays in Honour of A. F. J. Klijn* (Kampen, 1988) pp. 91–110, and C. D. Edsman, *Le baptême de feu* (Uppsala, 1940) pp. 182–89.
6. E.g. Aphrahat, *Demonstation* 6:1, 'Let us put on wedding garments'; *Virginity* 33, response, 'Hold me too, Lord, worthy to enter your glorious bridal chamber with your garments'. For bridal imagery see further below, Chapter Seven.

NOTES TO CHAPTER 6

1. For the Mesopotamian background to the phrase see G. Widengren, *Mesopotamian Elements in Manichaeism* (Uppsala/Leipzig, 1946) pp. 129–38. Among Greek writers, lgnatius' phrase 'medicine of immortality' (Ephesians 20:3) will come to mind.

2. This understanding is closely linked with the problem of how the 'three days' (Matthew 27:63–4) were to be counted; compare already Aphrahat, *Demonstration* 12:6- 7.

3. Thus in *Discourse on our Lord* 48 'Christ is a coal of fire hidden in flesh'; cp also *Commentary on the Diatessaron* 1:25; *Nativity* 6:13.

4. In general, see my 'Mary and the Eucharist', and (for the chronology of the Annunciation and the terminology) 'Passover, Annunciation and Epiclesis'.

5. This identification is already to be found in the second century, in the *Protogospel of James*.

6. For details, see my 'An early interpretation of *pasah*', in J. A. Emerton and S. C. Reif, *Interpreting the Hebrew Bible: Essays in honour of E. I. J. Rosenthal* (Cambridge, 1982) pp. 27- 34.

7. Ephrem plays on two meanings of *shra*, 'reside' (so verse ten), but also 'release, undo' (thus in verse nine).

8. See further my 'The lost Old Syriac at Luke 1:35 and the earliest Syriac terms for the Incarnation', in *Gospel Traditions in the Second Century*, ed. W. L. Petersen (Notre Dame, 1989) pp. 117–31, and for the later uses of *aggen* and derivatives in monastic literature '*Maggnanuta*: a technical term in East Syrian spirituality and its background', in *Mélanges A. Guillaumont. Contributions à l'étude des christianismes orientaux*, Cahiers d'Orientalisme 20 (1988) pp. 121–29.

NOTES TO CHAPTER 7

1. E.g. Aphrahat, *Demonstration* 6:1, 6; Ephrem, *Faith* 11:8; *Sermons* II.iv, lines 308, 328, 446.

2. Cp Murray, *Symbols*, chapter 1 'The Nation and the Nations'.

3. This is at least suggested by *Heresies* 39:9.

4. *Virginity* 20:9 unfairly says that only gentiles *(Aramaye)* gave praise (cp Murray, *Symbols*, p. 46, note 4).

5. For details, see 'Syriac dialogue poems', *Le Muséon* 97 (1984) pp. 48–49.

6. On these later texts, see H. Frank, 'Hodie caelesti sponso iuncta est ecclesia', in A. Mayer, J. Quasten, B. Neunheuser, edd., *Vom christlichen Mysterium: Gesammelte Arbeiten zum Gedächtins von Odo Casel OSB* (Düsseldorf, 1951) pp. 192–226; F. Graffin, 'Recherches sur le thème de l'Église-Epouse dans les liturgies et la littérature de langue syriaque', *L'Orient Syrien* 3 (1958) pp. 317–36.

7. *Soghitha* 5 in *CSCO* 186–7 = SS 82–3; English translation in Brock, *Sogiatha*, pp. 21–27.

8. *Homilies* 7–9 (in vol. I of Bedjan's edition).

9. There is a complete English translation of this hymn in my *The Syriac Fathers on Prayer and the Spiritual Life*, Cistercian Studies 101 (1987) pp. 36–38. Aphrahat gives a similar interpretation to Matthew 6:6 in *Demonstration* 4:10 (English translation in *The Syriac Fathers*, pp. 5–25).

NOTES TO CHAPTER 8

1. English translation in J. Gwynn, ed., *A Select Library of Nicene and Post-Nicene*

Fathers, II.13 (1898) pp. 362–75; Latin translation in *Patrologia Syriaca* I.

2. Besides the articles by Beck, Murray, and Vööbus cited in the Bibliography, the following are valuable: A. Adam, 'Grundbegriffe des Mönchtums in sprachlicher Sicht', *Zeitschrift für Kirchengeschichte* 65 (1953) pp. 209–39; A. Guillaumont, *Aux origines du monachisme chrétien*, Spiritualité orientale 30 (1979); F. E. Morard, 'Monachos, moine: histoire du terme grec jusqu'au IVe siècle', *Freiburger Zeitschrift für Philosophie und Theologie* 20 (1973) pp. 332–411; G. Nedungatt, 'The Covenanters of the Early Syriac- speaking Church', *OCP* 39 (1973) pp. 191–215, 419–44.

3. E.g. *Church* 17:8; *Heresies* 22:21.

4. The Peshitta, however, translates the phrase differently.

5. Compare the Macarian Homilies (ed. H. Berthold) LIV.4.5; and, at a further remove, note Philo's interiorized understanding of the passage in his *Allegorical Interpretation* II.49, where, after quoting Genesis 2:24, he says, 'For the sake of sense-perception the mind, when it has become her slave, abandons both God the Father of the universe, and God's Excellence and Wisdom, the Mother of all things, and cleaves to and becomes one with sense-perception and is resolved into sense-perception so that the two become one flesh and experience'.

6. *Patrologia Graeca* 23: col. 689B; the Jewish Greek translator Symmachus has *monachos* here in the sense of 'celibate'. For an earlier (AD 324) non-literary occurrence of *monachos* in the sense 'monk', see E. A. Judge, 'The earliest use of *monachos* for the monk', *Jahrbuch für Antike und Christentum* 20 (1977), pp. 72–89.

7. Eusebius, *Ecclesiastical History*, II.17.

8. E.g. *Commentary on the Pauline Epistles* (on 1 Timothy 4), p. 241 (text) = p. 250 (transl.).

9. There is also a wakefulness which is counterproductive, when it is put to bad purposes, as Ephrem points out in *Nativity* 1:77–78:

> If someone is wakeful, but not for chaste reasons,
> his wakefulness is sleep;
> if someone is wakeful, but impurely so,
> then his vigil is counterproductive.
> For there is a vigil that belongs to envy
> whose fill is utter loss;
> this sort of wakefulness is a merchandise
> that is full of mockery and derision.

NOTES TO CHAPTER 9

1. But also in some Greek (and Latin) writers.

2. Basil, *On the Holy Spirit* 29, and Homily II.6 on the *Hexaemeron*. The anonymous 'Syrian' (who is probably Eusebius of Emesa) was already wrongly identified as Ephrem before the middle of the fifth century by Sozomen, *Ecclesiastical History*, III.16; see further H. Lehmann, 'El Espiritu de Dios sobre las aguas. Fuentes de los comentarios de Basilio y Agustin sobre el Genesis 1,2', *Augustinus* 26 (1981) pp. 127- 39. For Basil and Ephrem, see

O. Rousseau, 'La rencontre de S. Ephrem et de S. Basile', *L'Orient Syrien* 2 (1957) pp. 261–84, and 3 (1958) pp. 73–90.

3. Ed. Jaeger, V:415–6; English translation quoted form J. Danièlou and H. Musurillo, *From Glory to Glory: Texts from Gregory of Nyssa's Writings* (New York, 1961) p. 129.

4. The issue of the incomprehensibility of God lay at the very centre of the controversy between Eunomius and the Anomoeans on the one side, and Basil and Gregory on the other. Basil's words in his work against Eunomius (I.14; PG 29: col. 545A), 'It is not the investigation of what God is, but the confession that he is, which provides us with salvation', echoes Ephrem's position exactly.

5. See for example Gregory's *Against Eunomius* (ed.Jaeger) II:228, 246, 302–4.

6. See now A. Louth, *Denys the Areopagite* (Wilton CT, 1989) pp. 79–81. Dionysius' commentary on the liturgy in the *Ecclesiastical Hierarchy* clearly has a Syrian background, and some contact with Syriac is suggested by his implicit pseudo-etymology of *diakonoi* as 'cleansers', a play on Syriac *mdakkyane* (*Ecclesiastical Hierarchy* V.1.6; Dionysius, however, avoids the term *diakonos* and uses *leitourgos* instead).

7. Gregory uses the imagery mainly in the context of the Song of Songs; for Ephrem, however, the New Testament references are of far greater importance.

8. There is a remarkable parallel in the Testament of Adam, Fragment II, 1 and 2: 'You wanted to be a god, a god will I make you', and 'I will make you a god, just as you wanted'. The work is of uncertain date.

9. *Nativity* 6:14 and 8:2 (compare the term *theanthropos* in Greek).

10. Compare also *Faith* 80:2–3.

11. *Memre on Faith* 3:31–2.

12. This is of course not the same as omniscience.

13. That is, a *monachos* in the pre-monastic sense, as found in the Gospel of Thomas (see Chapter Eight).

14. As a result a number of texts on monastic topics came to be ascribed to him (included among these are the early hymn cycles on Abraham Qidunaya and Julian Saba, published by Beck in CSCO 322–3 = SS 140–1).

15. See Chapter Four. For the subsequent use of the terms see *The Syriac Fathers on Prayer*, pp. xxviii–xxxi.

16. E.g. Sahdona (ed. de Halleux), I, p. 100. It is not of course confined to Syriac writers; among Greek authors, e.g. Hesychius of Sinai, in *P.G.*93: col. 1493C. See further my 'The spirituality of the heart in Syrian tradition', *The Harp* 1:2/3 (1987) pp. 93–115.

17. Isaac of Nineveh in particular has a remarkable passage on this (translated in *Novum Testamentum* 24 (1982) pp. 231–32, with some further references).

NOTES TO CHAPTER 10

1. There are of course some features in Ephrem's writings which are either of little or no contemporary interest, or which actually leave a bad taste in the modern reader's mouth; here I have in mind his unsympathetic attitude to the Jews: some of the epithets he uses of them will seem all the more

offensive today to the modern reader—above all the western reader who will not fail to have at the back of his mind the appalling history of European anti-semitism which climaxed in the holocaust. In the context of his own surroundings and the current rhetorical tradition of invective, however, Ephrem's hostility becomes more explainable, especially if there is anything in the recent suggestion that he already knew of the scurrilous Jewish tales alleging that Jesus was the offspring of a prostitute and a Roman soldier—tales which come down to us in the various recensions of the *Toledot Yeshu'*. But in any case it was not Ephrem's wish to see them consigned to Gehenna; rather he prays

> Lord, forgive sinners and those who have gone astray,
> the crucifiers too and those who have caused your servants to go
>   to their rest;
> grant them all rest in your Kingdom. (*Armenian Hymns* 45, end).

2. There may possibly be some traces of phraseology which goes back to direct oral tradition, but these are hard to identify; the term, *shra*, 'reside', used of the Word, may have such an origin (see the reference in note 8 to Chapter Six).

3. See note 1 to Chapter One.

4. For an analogous situation in the sciences, see note 7.

5. One might compare the approach advocated by A. Louth in his *Discerning the Mystery: An Essay on the Nature of Theology* (Oxford, 1983), especially Chapter V; Louth takes as one of his starting points H-G. Gadamer's *Truth and Method* (English trans., London, 1975). R. Murray has interestingly commented that Ephrem's 'defence of the symbolic method seems, to me at least, an extraordinary anticipation, by sixteen centuries, of the basic philosophical position of Paul Ricoeur' ('Theory of Symbolism', p. 3). A helpful essay by L. S. Mudge, 'Paul Ricoeur on biblical interpretation', can be found in Paul Ricoeur, *Essays on Biblical Interpretation* (London, 1981) pp. 1–40.

6. Compare *Heresies* 21:6, *Comm. Gen.* II.9, and *Prose Refutations* I, pp. lxxxv–lxxxvi.

7. F. Capra, *The Turning Point* (Fontana edition, London, 1983) pp. 66, 76.

8. Among the many basic points in common one might note in particular the rejection of determinism (p. 290) and the emphasis on complementarity (p. 309). A number of intriguing analogies would be worth exploring further: for example the relationship of historical to spiritual interpretation of Scripture could be compared to the relationship between classical and subatomic particle physics: the two members of each pair operate in a totally different (but not mutually exclusive) manner, and are subject to different modes of time—historical and linear time in the case of historical interpretation and classical physics, and sacred time and 'space-time' in the case of spiritual interpretation and particle physics. Likewise there would appear to be some interesting intimations of a Jungian approach to psychology: thus, for example, Ephrem's use of Adam typology functions as a way of describing the means for healing the collective unconscious, while his insistence on an attitude of engagement fits in with Jung's insight that psychotherapy can

only come from a personal encounter between therapist and patient (see also Louth's exposition, based on Gadamer, in *Discerning the Mystery*, pp. 29–41).

9. Capra, p. 330. In passing it should be noted that Capra's one-sided view of the Judaeo-Christian tradition has led him to overlook any possible contribution it might offer to the debate.

10. Ed. P. Bedjan, *Acta Martyrum et Sanctorum* (Paris/Leipzig, 1892) III:668.

11. Ed. Bedjan, III:672.

12. The anonymous Syriac poem is published, with English translation, in *Le Muséon* 99 (1986) pp. 61–129 (esp. 122–9); see also my 'Reading between the lines: Sarah and the Sacrifice of Isaac', in *An Illusion of the Night: Women in Ancient Societies*, ed. L. Archer, S. Fischler and M. Wyke (London, 1992).

13. E.g. *Resurrection* 1:7, *Nativity* 4:143. Compared to other early Syriac writers Ephrem does not make particular use of the feminine aspects of the Spirit; cp Murray, *Symbols*, pp. 142–44, and my 'The Holy Spirit as feminine in early Syrian tradition', in *Women, Theology and the Christian Tradition*, ed. J. Martin Soskice (London, 1990), pp. 73–88.

14. For the imagery of the 'breasts', compare *Memra on Faith* 1:267, *Heresies* 13:7.

15. Murray, *Symbols*, p. 31.

16. *Lausiac History*, Chapter 40 (Syriac translation published in CSCO 398–9 = SS 173–4). The Syriac insertion is also to be found in the *Apophthegmata* (Sayings of the Desert Fathers).

SELECT BIBLIOGRAPHY

The select bibliography is arranged as follows:

    A. Main texts and translations
    B. General: encyclopedia articles etc.
    C. Monographs
    D. Articles

Under C and D reasonably full coverage is given of recent works which deal with themes relevant to the study of Ephrem's spirituality.

The following abbreviations are used:

CSCO	Corpus Scriptorum Christianorum Orientalium (in each pair of volumes the first contains the text and the second the translation)
ECR	*Eastern Churches Review*
Gwynn	(see A.5)
HS	*Harp of the Spirit* (see below, A.5)
McVey	(see A.5)
Morris	(see A.5)
OC	*Oriens Christianus*
OCA	*Orientalia Christiana Analecta*
OCP	*Orientalia Christiana Periodica*
PdO	*Parole de l'Orient*
PO	*Patrologia Orientalis*

SCh   *Sources chrétiennes*
SA   Scriptores Armeni (in CSCO)
SS   Scriptores Syri (in CSCO).

A. MAIN TEXTS AND TRANSLATIONS (Language of translation in brackets)

1. PROSE WORKS

Commentary on Genesis and Exodus: CSCO 152–3 = SS 71–72 (Latin); an unpublished English translation by K. Refson is on deposit in the Bodleian Library, Oxford (M.Litt. thesis, 1982); Spanish by A. Peral Torres. Madrid, 1978.

Commentary on the Diatessaron: CSCO 137, 145 = SA 1–2 (Latin), and L. Leloir, *Saint Ephrem, Commentaire de l'Évangile concordant*. Dublin, 1963 (Latin); SCh 121 (French). Extensive further fragments are now published by L. Leloir, *Saint Ephrem, Commentaire de L'Évangile Concordant. Folios additionels*. Leuven, 1990 (Latin).

Commentary on Acts and the Pauline Epistles, preserved only in Armenian: Latin of the former in F. J. Foakes Jackson and K. Lake, *The Beginnings of Christianity*, 3. London, 1926, and of the latter by the Mekhitarist Fathers. Venice, 1893.

Polemical works: C. W. Mitchell, *S. Ephraim's Prose Refutations*, two vols. (English). London, 1912, 1921.

2. ARTISTIC PROSE

Homily on Our Lord: CSCO 270–1 = SS 116–7 (German); English in Gwynn.

Letter to Publius: *Le Muséon* 89 (1976) (English).

3. VERSE - MADRASHE

Hymns on Faith (eighty-seven hymns): CSCO 154–5 = SS 73–4 (German); English in Morris (A.5). More recent English translations of nos 14, 73, and 82 are in *HS* (A.5); of nos 10 and 20 in *ECR* and *PdO* 6/7 (by R. Murray; see also note 7 to Chapter Two, and note 9 to Chapter Seven), and of no 18 in *ECR* 10 (by P. Yousif). An important study by E. Beck appears in *Studia Anselmiana* 21 (1949).

Hymns on Nisibis (seventy-seven hymns): CSCO 218–9, 240–1 = SS 92–3, 102–3 (German); English of nos 1–21, 35–42 and 52–68 in Gwynn (A.5), and of nos 36, 50, 52, and 69 in *HS*.

Hymns against Heresies (fifty-six hymns): CSCO 169–70 = SS 76–7 (German).

Hymns on Virginity (fifty-two hymns): CSCO 223–4 = SS 94–5 (German); French of nos 8– 11 (by P. Yousif) in *PdO* 8; English of no 31 (by R. Murray) in *Sobornost/ECR 1* (1979), and of nos 7 and 33 in *HS*; Spanish of nos 4–8 (by F. J. Martinez) in *Compostellanum* 32 (1987). Complete translation in McVey (A.5).

Hymns on the Church (fifty-two hymns): CSCO 198–9 = SS 84–5 (German); English of n. 9 (by R. Murray) in *Sobornost/ECR 2* (1980), and of n. 36 (by S. P. Brock) in *ECR* 7 (1976).

Hymns on the Nativity (twenty-eight hymns): CSCO 186–7 = SS 82–3 (German); English of most of these is in Gwynn (with different numbering), and of n. 11 in *HS*. The same volumes of CSCO contain thirteen hymns of Epiphany, most of which are not by Ephrem (English in Gwynn). Complete translation in McVey.

Hymns on Unleavened Bread (twenty-one hymns), on the Crucifixion (nine hymns), and on the Resurrection (five hymns): CSCO 248–9 = SS 108–9 (German); an English translation of H. Azym. 3 is in *PdO* 6/7 and *HS*; the English of H. Res. 1–2 is in *HS*; the French (by B. Outtier) of H. Azym 1–2 is in *PdO* 6/7. Studies by J. Gribmont in *PdO* 4, and by G. Rouwhorst (with French translation) are in *Vigiliae Christianae, Supplement* 7 (1989).

Hymns on Paradise (fifteen hymns): CSCO 174–5 = SS 78–9 (German); French in *SCh* 137; English by S.P. Brock (1990). English of no 5 in *HS*; Latin, with commentary, in *Studia Anselmiana* 26 (1951) (by E. Beck).

Hymns on the Fast (ten hymns); CSCO 246–7 = SS 106–7 (German); English of no 6 in *HS*.

Hymns against Julian (four hymns); CSCO 174–5 = SS 78–9 (German); English by S. N. C. and J. Lieu, *The Emperor Julian* (Liverpool, 1986), and in McVey.

Hymns preserved only in Armenian (fifty-one hymns): *PO* 30 (Latin). English of no 49 in *HS* and of 46 (by R. Murray) in *Sobornost/ECR* 11 1989; French of three hymns on the Eucharist (by L. Mariès) in *Recherches de Sciences Religieuses* 42 and 45, of nos 2–7 and 9 (by F. Graffin) in *L'Orient Syrien* 6 (1961), and of 47–51 (by B. Outtier) in *Lettre aux amis de Solesmes* 1979–82.

4. VERSE - *MEMRE*

Six Homilies on Faith: CSCO 212–3 = SS 88–9 (German); English in Morris. Study by E. Beck in *Studia Anselmiana* 33 (1953).

Sixteen Homilies on Nicomedia (complete only in Armenian): *PO* 37 (French).

Numerous *memre* are attributed to Ephrem, but only a few of these are likely to be genuine, even among those published by E. Beck in CSCO 305–6 = SS 130–1 (*Sermones* I); CSCO 311–2 = SS 134–5 (*Sermones* II); CSCO 320–1 = SS 138–9 (*Sermones* III); CSCO 334–5 = SS 148–9 (*Sermones* IV); CSCO 363–4 = SS 159–60 (Nachträge); and CSCO 412–3 = SS 181–2 (*Sermones in Hebdomadam Sanctam*), all with German translation.

5. TRANSLATIONS OF SELECTED WORKS

E. Beck. *Ephräm der Syrer: Lobgesang aus der Wüste*. Freiburg, 1967.

S. P. Brock. *The Harp of the Spirit: Eighteen Poems of Saint Ephrem*, Studies Supplementary to *Sobornost*, 4, 2nd ed. London, 1983.

A Garland of Hymns from the Early Church. Maclean, Virginia, 1989. (Includes the following hymns by Ephrem: *Par.* 1, *Fast* 3, *Church* 37, *Nativity* 17, *Faith* 8, 10, 20, 31, 40, 49, 81 and *Nisibis* 41).

S. Euringer and A. Rücker. *Des heiligen Ephräm des Syrers ausgewählte Schriften*. Bibliothek der Kirchenväter 37, 61. Kempten/Munich, 1919, 1928.

J. Gwynn, ed. Selections translated into English from the Hymns and Homilies of Ephraim the Syrian, in A Select Library of Nicene and Post-Nicene Fathers of the Christian Church, series two, volume 13. Oxford/New York, 1898; rpt. Grand Rapids, n.d.

K. McVey. *Ephrem the Syrian.* Classics of Western Spirituality. New York/Mahwah, 1989.

J. B. Morris. *Select Works of St Ephrem the Syrian.* Oxford, 1847.

B. GENERAL: ENCYCLOPEDIA ARTICLES ETC.

E. Beck, in *Dictionnaire de Spiritualité* 4 (1960) 788–800; and in *Reallexikon für Antike und Christentum* 5 (1962) 520–31.

S. P. Brock, in *A Dictionary of Christian Spirituality.* Ed. Gordon S. Wakefield. London [- Philadelphia], 1983: 134–5; and 'Materials for the study of the writings of St Ephrem', in *Aufstieg und Niedergang der römischen Welt* (forthcoming).

————. 'A brief guide to the main editions and translations of the words of St. Ephrem', *The Harp* (Kottayam) 3 (1990) 7–29.

A. de Halleux. 'La transmission des Hymnes d'Ephrem d'après le ms. Sinai syr. 10', *OCA* 197 (1974) 21–63.

L. Leloir, in *Dictionnaire d'Histoire et de Géographie Ecclésiastique* 15 (1963) 590–7.

J. Melki. 'S. Ephrem le syrien: un bilan de l'édition critique', *PdO* 11 (1983) 3–88.

R. Murray, in *Catholic Dictionary of Theology* 2 (1967), 220–3; and in *Theologische Realenzyklopädie* 9 (1982) 755–62.

I. Ortiz de Urbina. *Patrologia Syriaca*, 2nd ed. Rome, 1965: 56–83. (A French translation, bringing this invaluable handbook up to date, is being prepared by R. Lavenant).

F. Rilliet, in *Dizionario di Patristica e di Antichita cristiana.* Rome, 1982: 1103–7.

J. M. Sauget, in *Bibliotheca Sanctorum* 4 (1964) 944–49. (For a full bibliography see *PdO* 4 (1973), supplemented (for the years 1971–80) by *PdO* 10 (1981/2) 320–7, and (for the years 1981–85) by *PdO* 14 (1987) 305–8.

C. MONOGRAPHS

E. Beck. *Die Theologie des hl. Ephraem in seinen Hymnen über den Glauben.* Studia Anselmiana 21. Rome, 1949.

————. *Ephraems Hymnen über das Paradies.* Studia Anselmiana 26. Rome, 1951.

————. *Ephraems Reden über den Glauben*. Studia Anselmiana 33. Rome, 1953.

————. *Ephraems des Syrers Psychologie und Erkenntnislehre*. CSCO 419 = Subsidia 58. 1980.

————. *Ephraems Trinitätslehre im Bild von Sonne/Feuer, Licht und Wärme*. CSCO 425 = Subsidia 62. Rome, 1981.

————. *Dorea und Charis. Die Taufe: Zwei Beiträge zur Theologie Ephräms des Syrers*. CSCO 457 = Subsidia 72. Rome, 1984.

T. Bou Mansour. *La pensée symbolique de saint Ephrem le Syrien*. Bibliothèque de l'Université Saint Esprit, Kaslik, 16. Kaslik, Lebanon, 1988.

S. P. Brock. *St. Ephrem The Syrian: Hymns on Paradise*. Crestwood, New York, 1990.

W. Cramer. *Die Engelvorstellung bei Ephraem dem Syrer*. OCA 173. Rome, 1965.

N. El-Khoury. *Die Interpretation der Welt bei Ephraem dem Syrer*. Tübinger theologische Studien 6. Tübingen, 1976.

S. Hidal. *Interpretatio Syriaca. Die Kommentare des heiligen. Ephraem des Syrers zu Genesis und Exodus mit besonderer Berücksichtigung ihrer auslegungsgeschichtlichen Stellung*. Lund, 1974.

T. Kronholm. *Motifs from Genesis 1–11 in the Genuine Hymns of Ephrem the Syrian*. Lund, 1978.

L. Leloir. *Doctrines et méthodes de S. Ephrem d'après son commentaire de l'Evangile concordant*. CSCO 220 = Subsidia 18. Rome, 1961.

J. Martikainen. *Das Böse und der Teufel in der Theologie Ephraems des Syrers*. Abo, 1978.

————. *Gerechtigkeit und Güte Gottes. Studien zur Theologie Ephraems des Syrers und des Philoxenos von Mabbug*. Göttingen, 1980.

W. L. Peterson. *The Diatessaron and Ephrem Syrus as Sources of Romanos the Melodist*. CSCO 475 = Subsidia 74. Rome, 1985.

G. A. M. Rouwhorst. *Les hymnes pascales d'Ephrem de Nisibe*. Supplement 7 to *Vigiliae Christianae*. 1989.

G. Saber. *La théologie baptismale de saint Ephrem*. Kaslik, Lebanon, 1974.

R. Terzoli. *Il tema della Beatitudine nei Padri Siri*, Chapter Five. Brescia, 1972.

P. Yousif. *L'Eucharistie chez saint Ephrem.* OCA 224. Rome, 1984.

Also relevant, but with wider coverage are:

S. J. Beggiani. *Early Syriac Theology with Special Reference to the Maronite Tradition.* Lanham, New York, 1983.

S. P. Brock. *The Holy Spirit in the Syrian Baptismal Tradition.* Syrian Churches Series 9. Kottayam, India, 1979.

————. *The Syriac Fathers on Prayer and the Spiritual Life.* Cistercian Studies 101. Kalamazoo, 1987.

————. *Spirituality in the Syriac Tradition.* Moran Etho Series 2. Kottayam, 1989.

W. Cramer. *Der Geist Gottes und des Menschen in frühsyrischer Theologie.* Münsterische Beiträge zur Theologie 46. Münster i. W.,1979.

R. Murray. *Symbols of Church and Kingdom: A Study in Early Syriac Tradition.* Cambridge, 1975.

A. Vööbus. *History of Asceticism in the Syrian Orient* I-III. CSCO 184, 197, 500 = Subsidia 14/17, 81. Rome, 1958, 1960, 1988.

D. ARTICLES

E. Beck, 'Das Bild vom Spiegel bei Ephrem'. *OCP* 19 (1953) 5–24.

————. 'Die Eucharistie bei Ephrem'. *OC* 38 (1954) 41–67.

————. 'Le Baptème chez s. Ephrem'. *L'Orient Syrien* 1 (1956) 111–36.

————. 'Die Mariologie der echten Schriften Ephraems'. *OC* 40 (1956) 22–39.

————. 'Symbolum-Mysterium bei Aphraat und Ephrem'. *OC* 42 (1958) 19–40.

————. 'Asketentum und Mönchtum bei Ephräm'. *OCA* 153 (1958) 341–42. (French translation: 'Ascéticisme et monachisme chez s. Ephrem'. *L'Orient Syrien* 3 (1958) 273- 298.

————. 'Das Bild vom Sauerteig bei Ephraem'. *OC* 63 (1979) 1–19.

————. 'Techne und Technites bei dem Syrer Ephraem'. *OCP* 47 (1981) 295–331.

————. 'Das Bild vom Weg mit Meilensteinen und Herbergen bei Ephraem'. *OC* 65 (1981), 1–39.

————. 'Glaube und Gebet bei Ephraem'. *OC* 66 (1982) 15–50.

————. 'Zur Terminologie von Ephraems Bildtheologie', in M. Schmidt, ed. *Typus, Symbol, Allegorie bei den östlichen Vätern und ihren Parallelen im Mittelalter*. Eichtstätter Beiträge 4. Eichstatt, 1982: 239–77.

————. '*Besra* (sarx) und *pagra* (soma) bei Ephraem der Syrer'. *OC* 70 (1986) 1–22.

————. 'Zwei ephrämische Bilder'. *OC* 71 (1987), 1–23.

S. Bonian. 'St Ephrem on War, Christian Suffering and the Eucharist'. *PdO* 11 (1983) 157–65.

P. J. Botha. 'Antithesis and argument in the hymns of Ephrem the Syrian'. *Hervormde Teologiese Studies* 44 (1988) 581–95.

————. 'Christology and Apology in Ephrem the Syrian'. *Hervormde Teologiese Studies* 45 (1989) 19–29.

T. Bou Mansour. 'La liberté chez S. Ephrem le Syrien'. *PdO* 11 (1983) 89–156.

————. 'Étude de la terminologie symbolique chez s. Ephrem'. *PdO* 14 (1987) 221–62.

S. P. Brock. 'World and Sacrament in the Writings of the Syrian Fathers'. *Sobornost* 6:10 (1974) 685–96; reprinted in *Studies in Syriac Spirituality*. Syrian Churches Series 13. [Kottayam] 1988: 1–12.

————. 'The poetic artistry of St Ephrem: an analysis of H. Azym. III'. *PdO* 6/7 (1975/6) 21–8.

————. 'The poet as theologian'. *Sobornost* 7:4 (1977) 243–50; reprinted in *Studies in Syriac Spirituality*, 53–61.

————. 'The Mysteries Hidden in the Side of Christ', *Sobornost* 7:6 (1978) 464–72; reprinted in *Studies in Syriac Spirituality*, 30–40.

————. 'Passover, Annunciation and Epiclesis: some remarks on the term *aggen* in the Syriac versions of Luke 1:35'. *Novum Testamentum* 24 (1982) 222–33.

————. 'Mary in Syriac Tradition', in A. Stacpoole, ed., *Mary's Place in Christian Dialogue*. Slough, 1982: 182–91.

————. 'Clothing metaphors as a means of theological expression in Syriac tradition'. In M. Schmidt, ed. *Typus, Symbol,*

Allegorie bei den östlichen Vätern und ihren Parallelen im Mittelalter. Eichstätter Beiträge 4. Eichstatt, 1982: 11–40.

D. Bundy. 'Language and the knowledge of God in Ephrem Syrus'. *The Patristic and Byzantine Review* 5 (1986) 91–103.

I.-H. Dalmais. 'Saint Ephrem et la tradition spirituelle des églises araméennes', *Connaissance des Pères de l'Église* 26 (1987) 8–25.

R. Darling. 'The "Church from the Nations" in the Exegesis of Ephrem'. *OCA* 229 (1987) 111- 21.

A. de Halleux. 'Mar Ephrem théologien'. *PdO* 4 (1973) 35–54.

———. 'Saint Ephrem le Syrien'. *Revue théologique de Louvain* 14 (1983) 328–55.

N. El-Khoury. 'Willensfreiheit bei Ephraem der Syrer'. *Ostkirchliche Studien* 25 (1976) 60–66.

———. 'Gen. 1:26 dans l'interprétation de Saint Ephrem, ou la rélation de l'homme à Dieu'. *OCA* 205 (1978) 199–205.

P. Feghali. 'Protologie et eschatologie dans l'oeuvre de S. Ephrem'. *PdO* 9 (1979/80) 307- 12.

F. Graffin. 'L'Eucharistie chez s. Ephrem'. *PdO* 9 (1973) 93–121.

J. Gribomont. 'Le triomphe de Paques d'après s. Ephrem'. *PdO* 4 (1973) 147–189.

———. 'La tradition liturgique des hymnes pascales de s. Ephrem'. *PdO* 4 (1973) 191- 246.

———. 'L'eucharistia nel commentario di Efrem al Diatessaron'. *Parola, Spirito e Vita* 7 (1983) 205–14.

S. H. Griffith. 'Ephraem the Deacon of Edessa and the Church of the Empire'. In *Diakonia. Studies in Honor of R. T. Meyer.* Ed. T. Halton and J. P. Williman. Washington DC, 1986: 22–52.

———. 'Ephraem the Syrian's Hymns against Julian. Meditations on history and imperial power'. *Vigiliae Christianae* 41 (1987) 238–66.

I. Hausherr. 'La philosophie du nom chez saint Ephrem'. In his *Noms du Christ et voies d'Oraison.* OCA 157. Rome, 1969: 64–72. English translation *The Name of Jesus.* Kalamazoo, 1978.

A. Kowalski. 'Revestiti di gloria: Adamo ed Eva nel commento di S.Efrem a Gen. 2,25'. *Cristianesimo nella storia* 3 (1982) 41–60.

L. Leloir. 'La pensée monastique d'Ephrem le Syrien'. *Travaux de l'Institut Catholique* (Paris) 10 (1964) 193–206.

———. 'Le commentaire d'Ephrem sur le Diatessaron. Quarante et un folios retrouvés'. *Revue Biblique* 94 (1987) 481–518.

———. 'S. Ephrem: le text de son commentaire du sermon sur la montagne'. *Augustinianum* 27 (1988) 361–91.

K. McVey. 'St Ephrem's understanding of spiritual progress: some points of comparison with Origen of Alexandria'. *The Harp* (Kottayam) 1:2/3 (1988) 117–28.

J. Martikainen. 'Some remarks about the Carmina Nisibena as a literary and theological source'. *OCA* 197 (1974) 345–52.

R. Murray. 'Mary the Second Eve in the Early Syriac Fathers'. *ECR* 3 (1971) 372–84.

———. 'The lance which reopened Paradise'. *OCP* 39 (1973) 224–34, 491.

———. 'The theory of symbolism in St Ephrem's theology'. *PdO* 6/7 (1975/6), 1–20. French translation in *Lettre de Ligugé* 203 (1980) 7–25.

———. 'The characteristics of the earliest Syriac Christianity'. In N. Garsoian, T. Mathews and R. Thomson, edd., *East of Byzantium*. Washington, DC, 1982: 3–16.

G. Noujaim. 'Essai sur quelques aspects de la philosophie d'Ephrem de Nisibe'. *PdO* 9 (1979/80) 27–50.

———. 'Anthropologie et économie de salut chez s. Ephrem: autour des notions de *ghalyata, kasyata* et *kasya*'. *PdO* 9 (1979/80) 313–5.

I. Ortiz de Urbina. 'La Vergine nella teologia di S. Ephrem'. *OCA* 197 (1974) 65–104.

G. Saber. 'La typologie sacramentaire et baptismale de s. Ephrem'. *PdO* 4 (1973) 73–91.

M. Schmidt. 'Die Augensymbolik bei Ephrem und Parallelen in der deutschen Mystik'. In her *Typus, Symbol, Allegorie bei den östlichen Vätern und ihren Parallelen im Mittelalter*. Eichstätter Beiträge 4. Eichstatt, 1982: 278–301.

———. 'Das Auge als Symbol der Erleuchtung bei Ephräm und Parallelen in der Mystik des Mittelalters'. *OC* 68 (1984) 27–57.

J. Teixidor. 'Muerte, Cielo y Seol en S. Efren'. *OCP* 27 (1961) 82–114.

———. 'Le thème de la descente aux enfers chez s. Ephrem'. *L'Orient Syrien* 6 (1961) 82–114.

———. 'La verdad de la resurrección en la poesia de San Efren'. *Anales del Seminario de Valencia* 1 (1961) 99–124.

A. Vööbus. *History of Asceticism in the Syrian Orient* II. CSCO 197 = Subsidia 17. Leuven, 1960: 70–110.

———. 'Le reflet du monachisme primitif dans les écrits d'Ephrem le syrien'. *L'Orient Syrien* 4 (1959) 299–306.

J. Walsh. 'The Syriac Tradition: St Ephrem'. *The Way* 20 (1980) 228–33.

P. Yousif. 'Le croix de Jésus et le paradis d'Eden dans la typologie biblique de s. Ephrem'. *PdO* 6/7 (1975/6) 29–48.

———. 'L'eucharistie et le Saint Esprit d'après s. Ephrem de Nisibe'. In R. H. Fischer, ed., *A Tribute to Arthur Vööbus*. Chicago, 1977: 235–46.

———. 'Symbolisme christologique dans la Bible et dans la nature chez s. Ephrem de Nisibe. *PdO* 8 (1977/8) 5–66.

———. 'La vierge Marie et l'Eucharistie chez s. Ephrem'. *Études Mariales* 36/7 (1978/80) 49–80.

———. 'Histoire et temps dans la pensée de S. Ephrem de Nisibe'. *PdO* 10 (1981/2) 3– 35.

———. 'Typologie und Eucharistie bei Ephraem und Thomas von Aquin'. In M. Schmidt, ed. *Typus, Symbol Allegorie bei den östlichen Vätern und ihren Parlallelen im Mittelalter.* Eichstätter Beiträge 4. Eichstatt, 1982: 75–107.

———. 'An approach to the divine reality in the thought of St Ephrem of Nisibis'. In J. Madey and G. Kaniarakath, edd. *The Church I Love: A Tribute to Rev. Placid J. Podipara CMI* Kottayam, India, 1984: 54–69.

———. 'Marie et les derniers temps chez s. Ephrem de Nisibe'. *Études Mariales* 42 (1985), 31–55.

———. 'Exégèse et typologie bibliques chez s. Ehprem de Nisibe et chez s. Thomas d'Aquin'. *PdO* 13 (1986) 31–50.

———. 'Les formes littéraires du commentaire du Diatessaron de saint Ephrem'. *OCA* 229 (1987) 83–92.

INDEX OF BIBLICAL REFERENCES

Gen.	1:2	180	1Kgs.	18:38	38, 104
	2:22	80		21	165
	2:24	137, 179	2 Chr.	7:1	104
	2:25	87	Isai.	6:6	103
	3:7	88	Ps.	68:6	137
	3:8	33	Wis.	10:1	136
	3:16	103	Matt.	6:6	129, 178
	3:18	103, 165		9:15	115
	3:21	86–7		13:19, 23	156
	3:22	136		13:45	106
	3:24	80		15:27	40
	8:11	58		21:20–21	88
	8:17–18	134		21:33–41	118
	19:24	105		22:1–4	94, 115
	22:6	73		25:1–13	115, 121, 140
	31	170		25:13	140
	38	170		27:51	166
Exod.	12	57		27:63–4	178
	12:3	110		28:19	90
	12.7	113	Mark	2:19	115
	12:23	111	Luke	1:11	109
	17:6	83		1:35	110, 112, 171, 178
	19:10, 15	133–4			
	32	118		1:36	109
Num.	20:11	83		2:38	103
	25:7–8	83		3:5	71
1 Sam.	2	113		5:34	115

	8:15	71, 177		14:23	37
	11:26	26		19:34	80–4
	16:26	26	1 Cor.	6:19	36
	20:35–6	139–40		7:34	137
John	1:14	112		10:4	83
	1:18	171		11:29	105
	2	123		15:45	31
	2:21	111	2 Cor.	5	37
	3:29	115, 120–1		8:9	25
	5:35	121	Gal.	3:28	138
	8:17	41	Col.	2:14	81
	12:3, 7, 13	58–9	1 Tim.	4	179

INDEX OF PASSAGES IN EPHREM

HYMNS (*Madrashe*. Number and stanza: italicized references denote passages translated)

Hymns preserved in Armenian
(lines; but for hymn 49, stanzas)

6:42–7	*129*
45 end	*181*
47:13–14	*105*
47:27–30	*112–3*
47:46–7	*113–4, 128*
48:1–4	*82*
48:41–8	*102*
49:4	*83*
49:8	*82*
49:9–11	*100*

Hymns on the Church

2:18–23	*35–6*
3:9	*35*
5:1–2	171
11:4	71
13:5	35
17:8	179
24:3	70
25:18	*171–2*
28:17	*161*
29:1	*74*
29:9–10	*75*

30:1	*113, 172*
34:3	71
36:3–6	*91–2*
37	*71–3*
42R	89
49:7	*33*
51:8	*33*

Hymns on Crucifixion

1:2	*119–20*
3:9–10	*102*
5:11	31
8:2	137
8:13	*34*
9:2	*81*

Hymns on Faith

1	175
3:5	*71*
4:1	79
4:2	38
4:9	*55*
4:10	*56*
4:11	70
5:7	*66*

5:17	*154*	44:3	*63*
5:18	71	44:7	*41*
6:3	*54–5*	44:9–10	*68–9*
8:9	*27*	44:10	176
9:16	*27*	46:11	44
10:3	*57*	46:12	*64*
10:8	38, *104, 112*	49:4–5	*58*
10:9	79, *105*, 141	51:2–3	*28*
10:10	*104*	51:7	90
10:12	*105, 112*	52:1	176
10:13	38, *104*	53:12	71
10:17	*94, 108*	54:8	62, *65*
10:22	*40*	63:9–11	*64–5*
11:8	178	65:10–11	*69–70*
12:4	*20*	66:7	137
14:1–5	*124–5*	67:8	*47, 76*
16:5	*70–1*	69:11	*26*, 175
16:6–7	*78*	69:11–13	*67*
17:1	*68*	72:2	29
18:1	*79*	73	94
18:2	*79*	74:12	112
18:6	*59*	80:1	*69*
19:2	108	80:2–3	180
19:3	*108*	81:1	*106*
19:7	*28*	81:3	*106*
20:1–2	*129*	81:8	*106*
20:6–8	*130*	85:6–8	*107*
20:12	*45*		
29:1	*153*	**Hymns on the Fast**	
30:2	26	2:4	*31*
31:1–7	*60–2*	3:2	*88*
31:4	53	3:6	44
31:5	35	5:1	*123*
32:1	*43*		
32:2–3	*44*	**Hymns against Heresies**	
32:3	70	10:9	*166*
32:5	78	11R	34
32:9	*54*, 176	11:4	*35*
40	94	13:7	181
40:10	38, 176	17:5	*38, 93*
41:7	69	21:6	181
43R	44	21:8	176
44:2	*63*	22:21	179

24:6	*121*	*Hymns on Nisibis*	
26:6	*88*	16:1–4	*74–5*
28:9	*165*	16:6	54
28:11	*156*	16:11	*53*
29:35	141	36:1	*33*
30:4	*65*	39	83
32:9	*42–3, 156–7*	39:7	*83*
35:7	44	43:21	*95*
39:9	178	46:8	*99*
42:4	37	49:3	176
43:3	*37*	50:1	*45*
47:2	*37*, 108	50:5	45
50:4	*48*	52:1–6	*19*
		63:5	74
Hymns on the Nativity		69:12	*152*
1:13	99	76:6	19
1:43	*87–8*		
1:61–2	*140–1*	*Hymns on Paradise*	
1:77–8	*179*	3:8	*151–2*
2:9	176	5:2	*42, 164*
3:20	*111*	5:3–4	*163–4*
4:130	113	6:1	*45–6*
4:143	182	6:8	*100*
4:149–50	*172*	6:9	*96*
4:200	49	9:20	*153*
5:4	*90*	11:6	*47–8*
5:10	*113*	12:11	*39*
6:13–14	*103*	12:15–18	*150–1*
6:13	178	12:18	*34*
6:14	180		
8:2	180	*Hymns on the Resurrection*	
8:4	*82*	1:7	*171*, 182
8:18	*127*	3:1–2	*117*
9:2	37	3:2	*118*
11:2–3	*127*	3:3	*118*
11:6–8	*25*	3:4–5	*119*
12:2	90	3:7	*119*
13:2	*99*	4:10	*111*
16:11	*89*		
17:4	*89–90*	*Hymns on Unleavened Bread*	
21:4	140	1:10	105
22:39	*93*	3R	*80*
23:13	*85*	3:5–8	*57–8*

6:7	*110*	15:3	90
6:22	57	16:2	*123*
14:16	99	16:9	*87*
17:5	101	20:9	178
17:8–12	*101*	20:12	*42*
17:10	*89*	23:5	175
18:15	99	24:5	123
		25:16	125
Hymns on Virginity		30:10	*83, 166*
5:9	*121*	31:3	*99*
5:10	123	32:5	177
6:8	56	33R	*177*
6:9	175	33:4	*123–4*
7:3	*165–6*	37:2	*105–6*
7:10	*91*	44:20	*128*
7:13–14	58–9	48:15–18	*152–3*
9:12	57		

VERSE HOMILIES (*Memre.* Number and line)

On Faith		*On Nicomedia*	
1:267	182	3:191–2	*79*
3:31–2	180		
4:129–40	*63*		

PROSE WORKS

Commentary on Genesis		*Commentary on the Diatessaron*	
II:9	181	1:5	*103*
II:14	87	1:10–17	177
II:20	*149–50*	1:14	109
II:23	*149*	1:16	138
II:31	165	1:18–19	*50–1*
VI:12	*134*	1:25	178
XX:1	169	3:17	122
XXVIII:4	*170*	4:3	92
XXXIV	170	7:22	*49*
		16:10	*88*
Commentary on Exodus		21:5	*166*
XII:2–3	*109–10*	21:10	*84*

21:11	*81, 82*	*Letter to Publius*	
21:25	*96–7*	1–2	*76–7*
		22	159
Commentary on the Pauline Epistles			
(page of Latin tr.)		*Discourse on our Lord*	
62	37	1	178
68	*83–4*	3	19, 99
96	37	9	*88*
241	179	48	178
		55	*92*
Prose Refutations I	181		
Letter to Hypatius	*167*		

SYRIAC AND GREEK WRITERS

SYRIAC WRITERS OTHER THAN EPHREM

Anonymous
  *Dialogue Angel
  and Mary*   *54*
  *Dialogue John
  the Baptist and Christ*
  (Beck, Soghitha 5)   *122*
  *Dialogue Synagogue
  and Church*   *120*
  Hymns on Epiphany
  (attr. Ephrem)
    3:10   *38*
    4:8   141
    4:19–20   *93*
    5:12–14   177
    8:16   *138*
    12:1   *94*
    12:5   177
  Sermones (attr. Ephrem)
    II.iv   178

Aphrahat
  Demonstations
    4:10   178
    6   133
    6:1   177, 178
    6:4   137
    6:6   138
    12:6–7   178
    18:10   *137*
    21:13   117

Jacob of Serugh
  Homiliae
    II, p. 589   *177*
    III, p. 593   177
  Acta Martyrum et Sanctorum
    III, pp. 668, 672   *168–9,
    182.*

Testament of Adam   *180*

GREEK WRITERS

Athanasius   154

Basil
  Against Eunomius I.14   180
  On Hexaemeron II.6   179
  On Holy Spirit 29   179

Dionysius the Areopagite
  *Eccl.Hier.*V.1.6   180

Eusebius
  Comm. in Pss   137
  Eccl.Hist I.13   176
  II.17   138

Gospel of Thomas,
  Logion 75   139

Gregory of Nyssa
  *Comm. on Eccles.*III.7   *146*
  Against Eunomius
    II.228, 246, 302–4   180
    II.417–8   *146–7*

Ignatius
  to Ephesians 20:3   178

Palladius
  Lausiac History 40   *173–5,*
     182

Philo
  Allegorical
  Interpretation II.49   *179*

Plotinus
  Enneads I.6   148

Romanos
  Kontakion III
  on Resurrection   177

Sozomen
  Eccl.Hist. III.16   131,
     179–80

INDEX OF NAMES AND SUBJECTS

Aaron 153
Abgar 40, 176
Abraham 73, 117, 169
Adam 31–4, 53, 80–4, 91, 93–4, 96, 100, 126, 136, 139–40, 149–54, 165, 177, 182
Adam, Testament of 180
Addai, Teaching of 40
angels 26, 79, 105, 140
Anna (NT) 103
Anomoeans 16, 180
Anselm 29
Antony 136
Aphrahat 14–5, 117, 133, 135–8, 177–8
Aristotle 160
Arius, Arianism 16, 24
Ark 45, 58, 134, 153, 176
Athanasius 13, 15, 154
Awgen 132

Bacon, Francis 43
baptism, Christ's 29, 31, 85, 90–4
baptism, Christian 30–1, 39, 80, 86, 90–4, 107, 122–3
Bardaisan 16
Basil 13, 15, 17, 145, 155, 179–80
Beck, Dom E. 18, 132, 159

Benedict XV, Pope 159
Bethlehem 90
birthgiving (see conceiving)
Bishoi 17, 131, 155
Boaz 99
body 32, 36–8, 60, 93, 95, 125, 153
bridal chamber 113–4, 115–30
Bride 38, 115–30
Bridegroom 38, 115–30, 138, 147, 156

Cana 123–4, 127
Capra, F. 167–8
chasm, ontological 24, 26–7, 40–1, 67, 145
Church of Peoples, Nations 83, 119
clothing imagery 32–3, 39, 42, 46–8, 60–6, 85–97, 107
Coal of Fire 103–6
complementarity 33, 152
conceiving, birthgiving 39, 75, 89, 91, 129
Creator/created 26–7, 67
Cross (Tree, Wood) 31, 33, 58–9, 79–83, 177

Dante 173
David 90, 117

204

Death 19, 57, 59, 81
definitions (dogmatic) 23–4
Descent (to Sheol) 29–30
Dionysius the Areopagite 146–8, 180
dispute and dialogue poems 19, 54,
    120, 122
Dives 26
divinization 148–54

Eden 33–4, 47, 123
Edessa 16, 132
Egypt 57–8, 117, 131, 141, 154–5
Elijah 104
entry to Jerusalem 119–20, 122
epiclesis 108–9, 157
Eucharist 30, 37–8, 40, 79–80, 82,
    86, 99–114, 124–5, 157
Eunomius 16, 146, 180
Eusebius of Caesarea 21, 137–8, 176
Eusebius of Emesa 179
Evagrius 23
Eve 31–3, 53, 71–3, 80, 82, 86–7, 96,
    99, 126, 139, 149–50, 165, 177
Exodus 57–8, 80, 101
eye (inner) 39, 71–2, 77, 126
Ezekiel 71

faith 29, 69, 71, 78, 129–30
Fall 32, 53, 85–6, 165
feminine imagery 129, 137, 168–72
fire 38, 84, 93–4, 104–5, 108, 112
Flood 59, 134
fountain 44, 50, 82, 88, 106
freewill 31, 34–6, 54, 147, 149, 151,
    167
furnace 36, 39

Gabriel 54, 110
Gehenna 77, 147, 177
Golgotha 82, 102
Grace 47, 54, 113, 162, 165
Gregory of Nazianzus 13, 15
Gregory of Nyssa 13, 15, 145–8, 180

Hannah (OT) 113, 172
heart 73, 127–30, 156
hidden/revealed 27–9
hidden power 41, 55, 113, 162, 165
Holy Spirit 58, 63–4, 90, 92–3, 99,
    104, 108, 111, 113, 137, 145, 157,
    162, 170, 173

individual/collective 30–1, 125–6
interconnections 167–8
interpretation of the Bible 46–51,
    161–4
Isaac (OT) 73
Isaac of Nineveh 73, 180
Isaiah 103–4
Israel 116–9, 125

Jacob (OT) 170
Jacob of Serugh 84, 93, 122, 168, 177
Jephtha's daughter 74
Jerusalem 119–20, 122
Jews, Judaism 48, 57, 68, 176, 181
Jezebel 165
John of Apameia 156–7
John the Baptist 73, 120–2, 138
Jordan 31, 90–2, 94, 112, 122
Joseph (OT) 170
Judah (OT) 170
Julian (emperor) 16

Laban 170
Law 45, 48, 58
Lazarus 26
light 39, 69, 71, 91–2, 94
Lot 170
Love 45, 70, 130

Macarian Homilies 132, 156, 179
Mandaeans 86
Manichaeans 16, 21, 86, 139
manna 106
Marcion, Marcionites 16, 108, 139
marriage, wedding feast 34, 95, 115–6,
    123–5, 127

Mary 32–3, 38, 54, 56, 59, 71–3, 91–2, 94, 106, 108, 110–3, 126–7, 157, 165, 171–2
Mattai, monastery of Mar 133
Maximus the Confessor 148
medical imagery 35, 40, 88, 99
Medicine of Life 19, 40, 82, 99–114
Meir, Rabbi 87
mirror 39, 47, 59, 74–7, 129, 147
monasticism 131–41, 154–7
Moriah, mount 73
Moses 92, 99, 120, 125, 153, 164, 168
Murray, R. 173

names 42, 46, 60–6, 176
Nature 41, 49, 53–5, 59, 103, 156, 164–5
Nisan 33, 109, 111, 117, 119
Nisibis 16
Noah 35, 58–9, 134, 153

oil 58–9, 121–2
olive 58

Pachomius 136
Palladius 131, 155, 173, 175
Paradise 32–4, 77, 81, 83, 88, 96, 100–1, 116, 139–40, 150–3, 163
paradox 24–5
parrot 60–2
Passover 57, 101, 103, 110–1, 113, 119
Paul, St 83, 93, 96, 105, 137
pearl 56, 78, 106–8
Pharisees 115
Philo 137
Philoxenus 156
Phinehas 83
Pisoes (see Bishoi)
Plotinus 148
Potiphar's wife 170
praise 78–9, 124

prayer 70, 75, 129–30
Proclus 147

Qumran 134

Rachel 170
robe of glory 85–97, 149
rock 50, 83
Romanos 144, 169, 177
Ruth 99

Sahdona 180
Samuel 113, 172
Sarah 119, 169
Satan, Evil One 19, 23, 37, 39, 57, 75
Scripture (see also interpretation) 46–51, 53–5, 59, 76, 103, 156, 161–4
Shakespeare 32
Shekhina 111
Sheol 29, 92, 99
side of Christ, piercing of (see Biblical Index, John 19:34)
Sinai 116–8, 125–6, 128, 153
Solomon 104
Sozomen 131
symbols, types 41–2, 46, 53–84
Synagogue 120, 122

Tamar 170
Tantalus 152
Targum 20, 86, 110, 136
Therapeutai 138
Thomas, Gospel 139, 180
time (historical and sacred) 29–32, 95, 126
titles of Christ:
    Bread of Rest 110; Bridegroom 95, 119–24, 138; Bright One 91; Cluster of Grapes 102; Coal of Fire 103; Cup of Salvation 102; Daystar 91; Doctor 40; Exalted One 25; Fire of Mercy 104; Firstborn

95; Grape of Mercy 99; Heavenly Bridegroom 124; Hidden One 25, 28, 55; Holy One 74, 113, 127; King's Son 118–9, 130; Lamb 102; Light 91; Living Lamb 58; Living One 34; Lord of Nature 156; Lord of Symbols 156; Lord of Thunder 111; Luminous One 74, 106; Medicine of Life 40, 82, 99, 105, 107, 112; Merciful One 85; Mighty 25; Pearl 106–7; Planter of the Garden 100; Priest 102; Provisioner 25; Pure One 74, 118; Ray 55; Rich 25; Royal Son 103; Sacrifice 102; Sacrificer 102; Sailor 58; Second Adam 84; Shepherd of All 19, 25; Slain One 83; Splendorous One 25; Steersman 58; True Altar 102; True Lamb 57, 101; Unique Bridegroom 121; Wakeful One 140–1; Wheatsheaf 102; Whole Offering 102

Titus of Bostra 21
treasure, treasury 70
Tree of Knowledge 31–2, 149, 151
Tree of Life 32, 50, 81, 96, 100, 149, 150–1
Trinity 15, 37, 90, 94
Truth 45, 55, 74, 130, 165

Urfa (see Edessa)

virginity 89, 123, 135–41
Vologeses, bishop 16
von Harnack, A. 148
Vööbus, A. 132

wedding (see marriage feast)
womb 91–2, 171
wonder 43–4

Zachariah (NT) 73, 109

INDEX OF GREEK (G), HEBREW
(H) AND SYRIAC TERMS

(listed in order of English alphabet)

aggen ('overshadow, tabernacle') 110–2

anachoresis ('withdrawal'; G) 136

'aqqeb ('investigate') 26

autexousiotes ('freewill'; G) 147

'ayna ('eye') 73

beth ḥlula ('wedding feast') 116

beth meshtutha ('wedding feast') 116

bnay qyama ('members of the Covenant') 133–5, 137

brith ('covenant'; H) 134

bṣa ('pry into') 26

bthulta ('virgin') 133, 135, 137

dayraya ('monk') 136

diakonos ('deacon'; G) 180

episkiasei ('overshadow'; G) 110

esarkothe ('became incarnate'; G) 39

galyata ('things revealed') 27–8

gnona ('bridal chamber') 110, 116

gnophos ('darkness'; G) 147

gushma ('body') 153

ḥathna ('bridegroom') 130

ḥayla kasya ('Hidden Power') 41

ḥeruta ('freedom, freewill') 31, 34, 147

horoi ('definitions'; G) 23

ḥuṣpa ('cheek, impudence') 71

iḥidaya ('Only-Begotten, single-minded, single, solitary') 130, 133–41, 154

iqara ('divine glory') 111

'ire ('Watchers, Wakers, angels') 140

ituta ('divine Being') 28

kasyuta ('hiddenness') 27

kenpa ('lap') 171

kenuta ('right, justice') 20

kolpos ('bosom'; G) 171

ktaba ('the Book, Scripture') 41

kyana ('Nature') 41

lebba ('heart') 73

ma'amad ('watch'; H) 135

'mad ('be baptized') 107

madrasha ('stanzaic poem, hymn') 18

mdakkyana ('purifier') 180

melta ('Word') 170

memra ('poem in couplets') 18

meshḥa ('oil') 58, 121

middat ha-din/raḥamim ('measure of judgement, mercy'; H) 20

monachos ('monk'; G) 136–8

monogenes ('Only-Begotten;' G) 136

mshiha ('Christ, Anointed') 58, 121

mysteria ('Eucharistic Mysteries'; G) 41

naphsha ('soul') 153

pasah ('pass over, Passover'; H) 111

proairesis ('free choice'; G) 147

purshana ('discernment') 47, 68

qaddisha, qaddishuta ('holy, holiness; continent, continence') 133–5, 138, 140

qnoma ('self') 63

qushta ('truth, reality') 28

qyama ('covenant') 133–5

qyamta ('resurrection') 135

raza ('mystery, symbol') 41, 56, 162–3

ruha d-qudsha ('Holy Spirit') 170

sam balati ('medicine of life'; Akkadian) 19

sam hayye ('medicine of life') 19

shaphya, shaphyuta ('luminous, luminosity') 73–4, 156

shlihe ('apostles, stripped') 107

shra ('reside') 11–2, 171, 178, 181

shrara ('truth, reality') 28, 41

statio ('vigil, watch'; Latin) 135

tar'ita ('intellectual spirit') 153

taybuta ('Grace') 20

tehra ('wonder') 69

theosis ('divinization'; G) 66, 148, 154

typos ('type'; G) 41

'ubba ('womb, cavity') 171

yahad ('community'; H) 134

yahid ('single'; H) 137

yawnaye ('pagan Greeks') 17

CISTERCIAN PUBLICATIONS, INC.
TITLES LISTINGS

CISTERCIAN TEXTS

THE WORKS OF BERNARD OF CLAIRVAUX

pologia to Abbot William
ve Books on Consideration: Advice to a Pope
race and Free Choice
omilies in Praise of the Blessed Virgin Mary
he Life and Death of Saint Malachy the Irishman
ove without Measure. Extracts from the Writings
    of St Bernard (Paul Dimier)
he Parables of Saint Bernard (Michael Casey)
ermons for the Summer Season
ermons on the Song of Songs I - IV
teps of Humility and Pride

THE WORKS OF WILLIAM OF SAINT THIERRY

he Enigma of Faith
xposition on the Epistle to the Romans
he Golden Epistle
he Mirror of Faith
he Nature and Dignity of Love

THE WORKS OF AELRED OF RIEVAULX

ialogue on the Soul
he Mirror of Charity
piritual Friendship
reatises I: On Jesus at the Age of Twelve, Rule for
    a Recluse, The Pastoral Prayer

THE WORKS OF JOHN OF FORD

ermons on the Final Verses of the Song of
    Songs I - VII

THE WORKS OF GILBERT OF HOYLAND

ermons on the Songs of Songs I-III
reatises, Sermons and Epistles

OTHER EARLY CISTERCIAN WRITERS

he Letters of Adam of Perseigne I
aldwin of Ford: Spiritual Tractates I - II
ertrud the Great of Helfta: Spiritual Exercises
ertrud the Great of Helfta: The Herald of God's
    Loving-Kindness
uerric of Igny: Liturgical Sermons I - II
lung of Prüfening: Cistercians and Cluniacs: The
    Case of Cîteaux
aac of Stella: Sermons on the Christian Year
erlo of Wilton & Serlo of Savigny
ephen of Lexington: Letters from Ireland
tephen of Sawley: Treatises

MONASTIC TEXTS

EASTERN CHRISTIAN TRADITION

sa: The Life of Shenoute
yril of Scythopolis: Lives of the Monks of Palestine
orotheos of Gaza: Discourses
agrius Ponticus:Praktikos and Chapters on
    Prayer
e Harlots of the Desert (Benedicta Ward)

Iosif Volotsky: Monastic Rule
The Lives of the Desert Fathers
The Lives of Simeon Stylites (Robert Doran)
The Luminous Eye (Sebastian Brock)
Mena of Nikiou: Isaac of Alexandria &
    St Macrobius
Pachomian Koinonia I - III
The Sayings of the Desert Fathers
    Spiritual Direction in the Early Christian East
    (Irénée Hausherr)
The Syriac Fathers on Prayer and the Spiritual Life
    (Sebastian Brock)

WESTERN CHRISTIAN TRADITION

Anselm of Canterbury: Letters I - [III]
Bede: Commentary on the Seven Catholic Epistles
Bede: Commentary on the Acts of the Apostles
Bede: Gospel Homilies I - II
Bede: Homilies on the Gospels I - II
Cassian: Conferences I - III
Gregory the Great: Forty Gospel Homilies
Guigo II the Carthusian: Ladder of Monks and
    Twelve Mediations
Peter of Celle: Selected Works
The Letters of Armand-Jean de Rance I - II
The Life of Beatrice of Nazareth
The Rule of the Master

CHRISTIAN SPIRITUALITY

Abba: Guides to Wholeness & Holiness East & West
A Cloud of Witnesses: The Development of
    Christian Doctrine (D.N. Bell)
Athirst for God: Spiritual Desire in Bernard of
    Clairvaux's Sermons on the Song of Songs
    (M. Casey)
Cistercian Way (André Louf)
Fathers Talking (Aelred Squire)
Friendship and Community (B. McGuire)
From Cloister to Classroom
Herald of Unity: The Life of Maria Gabrielle
    Sagheddu (M. Driscoll)
Life of St Mary Magdalene and of Her Sister St
    Martha (D. Mycoff)
The Name of Jesus (Irénée Hausherr)
Penthos: The Doctrine of Compunction in the
    Christian East (Irénée Hausherr)
Rancé and the Trappist Legacy (A.J. Krailsheimer)
The Roots of the Modern Christian Tradition
Russian Mystics (S. Bolshakoff)
The Spirituality of the Christian East (Tomas
    Spidlék)
Tuning In To Grace (André Louf)

MONASTIC STUDIES

Community & Abbot in the Rule of St Benedict
    I - II (Adalbert De Vogüé)
Beatrice of Nazareth in Her Context (Roger
    De Ganck)
Consider Your Call: A Theology of the Monastic
    Life (Daniel Rees et al.)
The Finances of the Cistercian Order in the Four
    teenth Century (Peter King)
Fountains Abbey & Its Benefactors (Joan Wardrop)

TITLES LISTINGS

The Hermit Monks of Grandmont (Carole A. Hutchison)

In the Unity of the Holy Spirit (Sighard Kleiner)

Monastic Practices (Charles Cummings)

The Occupation of Celtic Sites in Ireland by the Canons Regular of St Augustine and the Cistercians (Geraldine Carville)

The Rule of St Benedict: A Doctrinal and Spiritual Commentary (Adalbert de Vogüé)

The Rule of St Benedict (Br. Pinocchio)

Towards Unification with God (Beatrice of Nazareth in Her Context, II)

St Hugh of Lincoln (D.H. Farmer)

Serving God First (Sighard Kleiner)

CISTERCIAN STUDIES

A Difficult Saint (B. McGuire)

A Second Look at Saint Bernard (J. Leclercq)

Bernard of Clairvaux and the Cistercian Spirit (J. Leclercq)

Bernard of Clairvaux: Man, Monk, Mystic (M. Casey) Tapes and readings

Bernard of Clairvaux: Studies Presented to Dom Jean Leclercq

Christ the Way: The Christology of Guerric of Igny (John Morson)

Cistercian Sign Language

The Cistercian Spirit

The Cistercians in Denmark (Brian McGuire)

The Cistercians in Scandinavia (James France)

The Eleventh-century Background of Cîteaux (Bede K. Lackner)

The Golden Chain: Theological Anthropology of Isaac of Stella (Bernard McGinn)

Image and Likeness: The Augustinian Spirituality of William of St Thierry (D. N. Bell)

An Index of Cistercian Works and Authors in the Libraries of Great Britian I (D.N. Bell)

The Mystical Theology of St Bernard (Etiénne Gilson)

Nicholas Cotheret's Annals of Citeaux (Louis J. Lekai)

The Spiritual Teachings of St Bernard of Clairvaux (J.R. Sommerfeldt)

Wholly Animals: A Book of Beastly Tales (D.N.Bell)

William, Abbot of St Thierry

Women and St Bernard of Clairvaux (Jean Leclercq)

MEDIEVAL RELIGIOUS WOMEN
Lillian Thomas Shank and John A. Nichols, editors

Distant Echoes

Peace Weavers

STUDIES IN CISTERCIAN ART AND ARCHITECTURE
Meredith Parsons Lillich, editor

Studies I, II, III now available

Studies IV scheduled for 1992

THOMAS MERTON

The Climate of Monastic Prayer (T. Merton)

The Legacy of Thomas Merton (P. Hart)

The Message of Thomas Merton (P. Hart)

Thomas Merton: The Monastic Journey

Thomas Merton Monk (P. Hart)

Thomas Merton Monk & Artist (Victor Kramer)

Thomas Merton on St Bernard

Thomas Merton the Monastic Journey

Toward an Integrated Humanity (M. Basil Pennington et al.)

CISTERCIAN LITURGICAL DOCUMENTS SERIES
Chrysogonus Waddell, ocso, editor

The Cadouin Breviary (two volumes)

Hymn Collection of the Abbey of the Paraclete

Two Early Libelli Missarum

Molesme Summer-Season Breviary (4 volumes)

Institutiones nostrae: The Paraclete Statutes

Old French Ordinary and Breviary of the Abbey the Paraclete: Text & Commentary (2 vol.)

The Twelfth-century Cistercian Psalter

The Twelfth-century Usages of the Cistercian Lay brothers

STUDIA PATRISITICA
*Papers of the 1983 Oxford patristics conference
edited by Elizabeth A. Livingstone*

XVIII/I Historica-Gnostica-Biblica

XVIII/2 Critica-Classica-Ascetica-Liturgica

XVIII/3 Second Century-Clement & Origen-Cappodician Fathers

XVIII/4 *available from Peeters, Leuven*

Cistercian Publications is a non-profit corporation Its publishing program is restricted to monastic texts in translation and books on the monastic tradtion.

North American customers may order these books through booksellers or directly from the warehouse:
Cistercian Publications
St Joseph's Abbey
Spencer, Massachusetts 01562
(508) 885-7011
fax 508-885-4687

British and European customers may order these books through booksellers or from:
Brian Griffin
Storey House, White Cross
South Road, Lancaster LA1 4QX
England

Editorial queries and advance book information should directed to the Editorial Offices:
Cistercian Publications
Institute of Cistercian Studies
Western Michigan University
Kalamazoo, Michigan 49008
(616) 387-8920

A complete catalogue of texts in translation and studie on early, medieval, and modern monasticism is availa at no cost from Cistercian Publications.

Carolin Overhoff Ferreira

Identity and Difference

Filmwissenschaft

herausgegeben von

Privatdozent Mag. Dr. Claus Tieber

Band 13

LIT